THEORIES OF SMALL GROUP DEVELOPMENT

Fifth Edition

RAYE KASS, Ph.D.

Published by:
The Centre for Human Relations and Community Studies
Concordia University
Montreal, Quebec, Canada

FACULTY OF
ARTS AND SCIENCE

Centre for Human Relations
and Community Studies

ISBN: 978-0-9810500-2-7

5th edition © 2015, 1st printing, 2015
© 2015 by Raye Kass, PhD

Centre For Human Relations and Community Studies
Concordia University
7141 Sherbrooke St. W, VE-225.01
Montreal, QC, Canada, H4B 1R6
Phone: (514) 848-2424 ext. 2273   Fax: (514) 848-2262
Email: CHRCS@concordia.ca   Web: www.concordia.ca/artsci/chrcs.html

To order more copies of this book:
Visit: www.concordia.ca/bookstore or
Email: bookstore@concordia.ca

To My Mother,
with much love and deep gratitude

PREFACE

The objective of this book is to enhance the understanding of small group behaviour with a view to facilitating leadership intervention and task accomplishment in groups and teams, in the workplace as well as in social, therapeutic and educational settings.

The underlying assumption is that task accomplishment within a group can be greatly enhanced when those giving leadership have an understanding of the **developmental aspects of group process and the nature of group dynamics.** This understanding would not only influence the design, format and timing of learning experiences, but also the development and implementation of strategies, skills and norms within groups and teams.

As a professor researching small group behaviour and as a trainer of professionals involved in giving leadership in small groups, teams, committees, and so on, it has become abundantly clear to me over the past 30 years that leadership in small groups can be rendered more effective if guided by a framework of group development theory. My goal in writing this book is to provide such a framework.

I have chosen five key theories of group development used frequently and regularly by those studying leadership and small group behaviour. These theories have been tested out and used by hundreds of students and professionals under my supervision and training. They have been chosen specifically for their clarity, practicality and transferability, cutting across a range of contexts and holding true under varied conditions of composition, size, duration, and focus. Responsibility for these theories' factual accuracy rests completely with me. These particular theories are useful in that they contribute to the understanding of group process at each stage of a group's development. They also explain shifts in work level and they provide insights as to how groups get blocked and into the dynamics behind the inescapable influence of a group's emotional underworld.

The 5th edition of this book has a new chapter that has been added. This reflects current trends that influence the dynamics in groups, namely diversity, emotional intelligence and the digital age.

Raye Kass, Ph.D.
Concordia University
Montreal, Quebec
April 2015

TABLE OF CONTENTS

SECTION I

FIVE THEORIES OF SMALL
GROUP DEVELOPMENT

Although the scientific investigation of group work is but a few years old, I don't hesitate to predict that group work - that is, the handling of human beings not as isolated individuals, but in the social setting of groups - will soon be one of the most important theoretical and practical fields... there is no hope for creating a better world without a deeper scientific insight into the ... essentials of group life.

-Kurt Lewin (1943)

I. BION'S WORK AND EMOTION THEORY OF GROUP DEVELOPMENT

OVERVIEW

British psychoanalyst Wilfred Bion, during the late 40's developed a structure for understanding groups and group dynamics. His study was a result of working with psychiatric patients who were psychological casualties from World War II. The focus of these groups was known as "study groups" in which patients learned about themselves through group process and exploration of intra-group tensions. Bion, who meticulously recorded his sessions, noted the emergence of a two-level operation within the group: one dealing with the work level and the other with the emotional. He further distinguished three emotional modes: **dependency, fight-flight and pairing**. He argued that at any point in a group, there is some level of work going on with an under-current of one or another of these emotional modes.

Bion's framework for group work, while tested and used in a variety of settings, did not have much impact on the North American continent. However, his influence in England and Europe was such that his theories formed the basis for the current group work practice at Tavistock, England. In the late fifties, his theories gained prominence in the United States when they were used as a basis for further study by Stock and Thelen (1958) and expanded into a phase theory of group development by Bennis (1964).

Three distinctive characteristics are central to understanding Bion's work and emotion theory of group development:

1. **Emphasis on the process of the total group versus the individual.**
   Individual behaviour is seen and interpreted as an expression and representation of the group as a whole. Any comments made by an individual are seen to reflect concerns that are shared by the group.

2. **Emphasis on a rigid and specified leadership role and structure.**
   The leader restricts interventions to interpretations that uncover the covert, gives no advice, withholds opinions and is careful not to step out of role. The more nurturing role commonly associated with the leader is visibly absent.

3. **Emphasis on member responsibility and freedom to learn.**
   Individuals are responsible for their own actions and their own choices. Members can choose to learn or not to learn. The decision rests with them.

These distinguishing features represent the Tavistock approach to working with groups and set the stage for understanding Bion's framework of group process and development. This is a complex and exciting model that explains (a) the swing in shifts in the work level of a group, (b) how groups get stuck, and (c) the inescapable influence of the group's emotional underworld. In the following pages, I will elaborate on the three emotional modes of: dependency, fight-flight, and pairing, the coexisting aspects of work and emotion in groups, and the phases and sequences likely to occur in the life of a group.

```
┌──────────────────────────────────────────────┐
│                  DEPENDENCY                    │
│  Group relies on an authority figure or an     │
│  individual in the group to guide and          │
│  direct them. This could also be in the        │
│  form of creating policies, developing a       │
│  new idea, or a new way of doing things.       │
└──────────────────────────────────────────────┘
```

Dependency

Looking for direction,
guidance, and structure

Relying on external
authority

Counterdependency

Rejecting authority

Resisting suggestions
and outside influence

Creating an appearance
of independence

The central assumption in this mode is the belief that unless the group is led by an authority figure, it cannot function effectively. In fact, the success of the group is seen to depend on being led. It is with this perspective that the group looks to the leader for guidance and security, wanting her/him to solve their problems. If the leader refuses to comply, members may turn in anger and frustration toward each other rather than tackle the issue at hand.

Dependence does not necessarily mean reliance on a person, e.g., leader, teacher, trainer, consultant, etc. It could also mean reliance on a thing external to membership, e.g., resources, experts, policies, regulations, artefacts, surroundings, etc. Reliance on something external to membership is not unusual. Groups have been known to become so dependent on certain kinds of resources that their removal has rendered them helpless and confused.

During this dependency mode listening is low, cooperation is minimal, and feedback is practically non-existent. Any help offered by group members is usually ignored or sat upon. Assumptions pass unchallenged as statement of facts, and critical judgement is almost entirely absent. In fact, what we have is a group in which members do not typically have relationships with each other, however, each member has a relationship with the leader.

We note that during this dependency mode, group members are very conscious of the leader. What he/she does or says does not go unnoticed, and what he/she does not say or do takes on proportions of significance. This is so, whether the group is in a dependent or counterdependent mode. In fact, very little is done without members first checking it out with the leader. Approval is critical, and when it is not forthcoming, it is devastating. Measurement of success is not so much what one has accomplished, but approval by the leader. Here, recognition by the authority figure is critical; without it, members experience a sense of failure or feelings of inadequacy.

During this dependency mode, members are unwilling and reluctant to learn from each other. Their dependency is such that the notion that one can learn anything of value from a peer member is inconceivable. The leader is seen as the person with all the knowledge and all the expertise. It is not uncommon to see the group during this period unable to comprehend the simplest instructions or information, or unwilling to take on the simplest task without repeatedly checking for affirmation and approval. Risk-taking is very rarely experienced here, for it involves venturing outside the realms of safety - a situation difficult to envision, let alone enter when members are experiencing high dependency needs.

The group enters into a counterdependent mode when its members want to manipulate the leader to lead, or when members with a counterdependent tendency are able to shift the culture to that end of the polarity. Counterdependence here is seen as a stance indicating the rejection of the authority figure. This rejection is in the form of a denial as to the leader's abilities or even as to the leader's presence. Members may play down ideas or opinions offered by the leader. The group, while saying nothing, colludes in ignoring the leader's presence and excludes him/her from discussion. We also note that roles formerly taken by the leader are taken over by power members in the group. The energy in this counterdependent mode is given to carefully studied forms of rejection of authority or denial of outside influence. The concerted and deliberate effort in this direction is such, that its very rejection or denial suggests the overwhelming recognition of its presence.

Rioch (1970) points out the "childlike dependency" characteristic of this mode, describing group members as "perpetuating a state appropriate to an earlier stage of development," where they would generally much rather depend on the leader to tell them what to do than determine that for themselves. She notes the struggle that group members experience between "resentment at being in a dependent state" as well as a concomitant "desire to persist in it." It is this "childlike dependency" state that makes the outside world look cold and unfriendly to the group during this mode, and which makes members "close ranks and snuggle up to each other," giving the group a temporary, if not false, sense of security and comfort.

Of the three emotional modes, that of dependency is the most devastating to group building. The difficulty lies in the fact that the group needs to experience its own helplessness before it can begin to appreciate and build on its own resources. What is difficult to combat is the debilitating period of helplessness. Unless the group has learned to grow out of this dependency, it risks rapidly slipping back into it, even though this regression does nothing to enhance its maturity.

The period of dependency is a difficult one for both members and the leader. For members, the experience of having a leader who does not conform to what is expected or to what is familiar, catapults them into a state of disequilibrium. On the one hand, group members know that the leader is knowledgeable. On the other hand, there is some question as to her/his capabilities as these do not appear forthcoming. In fact, what the group experiences is a leader who is shirking his/her responsibilities. When this is experienced, it is not uncommon for the group to try to coax the leader to mend his/her ways and fall in with their wishes. Sometimes leaders feel impelled to make amends by responding to the exchange or by permitting some dependence to begin. However, for the leader who chooses not to enter the group's dependent mode, the struggle is to permit him/herself to be seen as a failure and in so doing, enable the group to develop its own resources. But there are no words that can prepare the leader for the "agonizing experience of the vilification" a group may heap upon his/her head, if he/she refuses to be "Big Daddy" (Peck, 1987). Peck contends that this issue calls into "question our very definitions of strengths and weaknesses." In other words, according to Bion (1961), the strong leader is the one who is willing to risk the accusation "mild or murderous" of failing to lead.

During this dependency mode, the style of leadership experienced by the group influences whether a power struggle evolves amongst members. Dimock (1987) notes that if the leader is "dominating and encourages dependence, the power struggle among the members is not as intense." However, a leader who is "permissive and group-centred" encourages the emergence of power struggle among members and counter-dependent behaviour towards themselves.

Typical Statements in the
Dependency / Counterdependency Mode

Dependency	Counterdependency
"We need someone to keep us on track as we discuss this issue."	"This doesn't apply to my situation. I don't work with people. I'm different."
"Why does he leave us floundering? Why doesn't he tell us what to do? He is the expert not we!"	"Don't tell me what to do. If I want help I'll ask for it."
"You seem to know so much. We really cannot go on without you."	"I propose that we do what we want, and to hell with the administration."
"She should be motivating us and telling us what to do, not asking us."	"Who does he think he is? We don't need his suggestions; we can get along very well without him."
"Do you think this is a good idea, or should we try for something else?"	"Sounds good, but has research really proved it."

FIGURE I-1

FIGHT-FLIGHT

The group acts as if its aim is to avoid some threat, stress, or anxiety by fighting or by running away from it. Action is seen as essential here.

Fight

Resisting stress and anxiety

Showing hostility towards other members and/or the leader

Flight

Fleeing stress

Avoiding confrontation

Seeking protection

Bion sees fight and flight as two sides of the same coin. The central assumption in this mode is that evasion and denial will best serve and preserve the group, or that attack and assertion are the best ways for the group to solve its problems. Members experience much stress during this period. The desire to reduce this stress either by fleeing from it or by confronting it, is quite high.

The group develops sophisticated ways of skirting issues, sidestepping critical decisions and postponing things that need to be addressed. It is not unusual during this state of flight, for members to engage in innumerable activities to circumvent the task at hand. Some of the many faces of flight are: whispering, joking around, chit-chatting, telling stories, coming late to the group, leaving early, absenteeism, scape-goating, by-passing, silence, silliness, engaging in irrelevancies, endlessly focusing on a topic that bears little relevance to the issue at hand, busily working at something that is unrelated to the focus of the group's goal, changing the subject, dodging emerging issues, talking about situations outside the room, and giving rapt attention for considerable time to a member who is focusing on irrelevant issues. Some groups develop a culture where food plays an important role serving a "compelling and interesting detour." Stock & Thelen (1958) suggest that although the group may say it is interested in working on a particular problem, its behaviour "seems to lead it farther and farther away from coming to grips with it."

On the other hand, fight is sometimes difficult to distinguish from work. Both require the mobilization of focussed energy. However, fight is not always directed towards confronting and dealing with the issue at hand, whereas, work is. When the group is in a fighting mode, verbal attack against members within the group or with the group leader is not unusual. Stock & Thelen (1958) suggest that when a group is in a fighting culture, one of its characteristics is that it "needs to attack something or someone."

9

Responsibility to mobilize the group is taken over by the power members with individual differences perceived as a threat to the group's survival. Feeble protests are swept aside by the more dominant members, with an underlying message of "tow the line or else." Resources and talents that are not readily perceived as useful to the survival of the group are ignored, negated, or wasted.

During this fighting mode, it is not unusual to see members engaging in challenging and questioning one another or the leader, thus participating in generalized criticism toward each other, or the group, and getting bogged down into "fruitless conflict" that involves trying to change someone. The hostility and aggression is directed to anyone (group member, leader, absent member) or anything (institution, other groups, policies) who present a threat to the survival of the group.

For some, this is an exciting, albeit stressful time, for others, it is a difficult period filled with hostility and anger, devoid of sensitivity, compassion and gentleness. During this mode there is much chaos, noise, squabbling, bickering, blaming, pressing for results, directing, sarcasm with almost any comment made by group members no matter how innocuous, calling for a hostile response. Here, dropping a stated idea or long held position is seen as giving in and labelled as weakness. Digging in one's heels becomes a virtue.

Action is essential whether the group is in a fight or flight mode. In fact, more than any other mode, the importance of a leader cannot be underscored for he/she is expected to either mobilize the group for attack or lead them into flight. What is important to note, is that during this mode, attack or flight offers "instantaneous satisfaction" and an immediate way to reduce anxiety and stress to group members. Whether in fight or in flight, enormous amounts of energy are expended by the group as it withholds or attacks.

Maintenance roles are defined as attention to relationships in the group. During this fight-flight mode, few maintenance roles are visible. In fact, what we have is a situation which works against "mutual assistance and satisfying work relationships" (Rioch, 1970). The group's need to preserve itself is so high, that there is little tolerance for an individual whose needs require a shift in focus from the group. The welfare of the individual becomes a matter of secondary consideration with the group abandoning the individual. Any concern shown by members for the welfare of the individual is discouraged and seen as out of place.

Similar to the dependency mode, where the designated group leader is expected to conform to a "stereotype image" of leadership, the leader who neither fights nor runs away is not easily understood or accepted.

Typical Statements in the
Fight-Flight Mode

Fight	Flight
"We've tried this one before; there is nothing more to gain from doing this again."	"I can't stand this any longer; let's do something, anything, as long as we do something!"
"We are wasting our time talking about this. Let's get on with it."	"Fine, this may work for others, but our group is different."
"I'm doing all right as I am, why change?"	"Same old stuff. I've seen and heard all of this before."
"We can't just sit around and wait for things to happen. Let's get out and do it."	"Count me out of this. I just came to watch, because I'm interested in the theory of group dynamics."
"Unless we take action now, we are unlikely to have much of a say in what happens later."	"Let's break into small sub-groups and talk about this."

FIGURE I-2

PAIRING

Group members turn to each other in pairs for support, closeness and acceptance. These alliances which may be conscious or unconscious detract from the cohesiveness of the large group.

Pairing

Moving toward intimacy, warmth and supportiveness

Counterpairing

Desiring isolation and distance

Engaging in impersonal interaction

The central assumption in this mode is that if an alliance can be built between two members in the group, a leader with special qualities who is able to create a safe environment given to unconditional acceptance, will emerge.

This desire to find or create a "haven in the midst of a heartless world" is not an uncommon occurrence. This is particularly evident in groups that have just come out of a difficult and stressful period. The desire for safety and the need for acceptance is such that group members turn to one another for contact and engage in a variety of pairing activities meant to create an atmosphere devoid of conflict and negative feelings. As with the emotional mode of flight, pairing takes on many faces such as: name dropping, flattering of status members, showing preferences, aligning oneself with those who have similar views, initiating the development of a subgroup or volunteering to join it, showing marked attention to certain members, stressing the common ground that exists between oneself and others and referring by name to certain members.

Bion views this kind of pairing as detracting from the cohesiveness of the large group, and as interfering with the development of maturity within it. Peck (1987) supports this notion, stating that the pairing mode is particularly counter-productive in groups designed to "build community among disparate groups" such as student and faculty, administration and staff, employers and employees, etc. He states that such subgroups begin by "sitting with one another as a block," often continuing to engage in excluding behaviour such as: whispering, giggling, and generally displaying a desire to remain separate by sitting apart and by making statements that draw attention to their distinctiveness.

"Pairing off" as perceived by Bion is quite dissimilar to Schutz's (1966) concept of "dyadic relations" and Gibb's (1964) concept of "protective pairing." With Schutz, dyadic relations, while clearly only occurring between pairs, is not an exclusive activity. The pair does not pull away and remains fully active in the group. With Gibb, while collusion occurs during the development of protective pairing, the movement towards pairs is seen as a basis for the development of trust. With Bion, the pairing off has an exclusive component to it. The dyads focus on their relationships to the exclusion of attention to the group. As long as hope and optimism prevail, the group "dotingly supports" such exclusive activity. However, the more active and intensive the pairing, the more likely schisms will eventually occur within the group.

When a group is in a counterpairing mode, members interact at arm's length and seem only comfortable on an intellectual plane. A rich array of behaviours is visible. Some of the more common ones displayed are: showing visible discomfort around closeness, displaying poor team spirit, and discouraging the expression of feeling. Moreover, we can perceive a denial of the need for inclusion, resistance to the development of sub-groupings, and the withholding of support and acceptance. Furthermore, we can also remark a display of behaviours as, ignoring invitations to join in, refusing favours, focusing on the "there and then" rather than the "here and now," shifting from the personal to the impersonal, drawing attention to differences, resisting the building on other's ideas and suggestions, and, finally, talking about feelings, rather than experiencing or expressing them.

Clearly, timing of when pairing and counterpairing take place is a critical factor to the group's development. If it occurs early in the life of the group and does not persist, it does not detract from the cohesiveness of the larger group. If however, it occurs later in the life of the group and does persist, it can and often does, undermine its process.

Typical Statements in the
Pairing-Counterpairing Mode

Fight	Flight
"Isn't this wonderful. We are having so much fun and it is so good for us." "Why don't we spend some time getting to know each other?" "I liked you the instant I saw you, and knew we would get along together." "I notice we have the same style of working. How about doing this part of the project together." "I know I'm in the right group, as several people here have similar interests to mine."	"It is so interesting to sit back and watch all these reactions. I'm learning so much." "Let's be objective. We need facts not feelings." "I'm really interested in joining the group on this activity, but I'm awfully busy and haven't had a moment to myself." "We don't have time for all this chit-chatting. Let's get down to work." "I prefer doing this on my own. It's faster and easier for me."

FIGURE I-3

Characteristic Features of Bion's Three Emotional Modes of Dependency, Fight-Flight and Pairing

Dependency	Fight-Flight	Pairing
Issues of competency begin to emerge.	Action is essential whether for fight or flight.	The timing when this occurs is critical to the group's development.
A strong leader is a person who is willing to risk the accusation of failing to lead.	The individual is of secondary importance to the preservation of the group.	If the pairing group is very active, there is a tendency for schisms within the group.
Style of leadership experienced by the group influences whether a power struggle evolves amongst members.	A leader is even more important than in any of the other emotional states, because the call for action requires a leader.	Pairing tends to detract from the cohesiveness of the larger group.
Marked inability on the part of individuals in the group to believe that they can possibly learn any-thing of value from each other.	Usually the person whose primary concern is the welfare of an individual is out of place.	Pairing is counterproductive in groups designed to build teams among previously disparate groups.
The tendency here is for individuals not to foster relationships with each other, but with the leader.	The behaviour in this mode often interferes with effective problem-solving.	The dyadic relationship makes it difficult for any individual to sustain dialogue with the group as a whole.

FIGURE I-4

Characteristic Features of all Three Emotional Modes of Dependency, Fight-Flight and Pairing

All Three Emotional States:

1. **Offer** instantaneous satisfaction.

2. **Represent** central assumptions that are **NOT** oriented toward reality.

3. Are **averse** to learning from experience.

4. **Interfere** with work.

5. **Focus** around the issue of leadership.

6. **Use language** filled with clichés, repetitive phrases and vague and loose generalizations.

7. **Attempt** to seduce the leaders away from their work function.

8. Do **not consider the consequence** of their activities and demonstrate little patience towards those with an inquiring attitude.

9. **Are disoriented about** time and display poor memory.

10. **Experience** central assumptions that are usually outside of the group's awareness.

FIGURE I-5

Adapted from Rioch (1970) and Yalom (1970).

KEY FEATURES OF BION'S THEORY

1. Emotional mode

2. Work mode

3. Relationship between work and emotion

4. Valency patterns

5. The individual and the group

6. Shifts in emotional modes

7. Phases of group development

8. Group formation

1.   Emotional Mode

As we can see, the emotional modes described earlier take on three different forms: dependency, fight-flight and pairing, **each of which involves basic assumptions about the group which have no basis in reality.** These central assumptions influence group behaviour. They are are briefly sumarized below.

Emotional Mode	Central Assumption
A. Dependency	The belief that unless the group is led by an authority figure it cannot function effectively.
B. Fight-Flight	The belief that evasion and denial will best serve and preserve the group, or that attack and assertion are the best ways to solve its problems.
C. Pairing	The belief that if an alliance can be built between two members in the group, a leader with special qualities who is able to create a safe environment, given to unconditional acceptance, will emerge.

These emotional modes and their associated assumptions are unconscious. They get activated as individuals enter into group situations. Since these are shared assumptions and since they are essentially outside of the group's awareness, they are easily denied and difficult to confront. These assumptions are powerful, and explain some of the ineffective and self-contradictory behaviours often observed in groups. Bunker (1974) suggests that when a group experiences one of these assumptions it tends to ignore its reason for existing, it deviates from its central focus, and abandons any form of rational behaviour. In short, the basic assumption serves to interfere with the work of the group.

2.   Work Mode

Central to understanding Bion's theory of group development is his concept of work. When is a group in a work mode? What does work mean within Bion's framework? What is the relationship between work and emotion?

According to Bion, a group is in a work mode when it is taking responsibility for carrying out its purpose. For example, in Bion's case, the members of his "study groups" at Tavistock met to learn about themselves through their understanding of how they function in a group. According to his definition, the group would be in a work mode if it were focussing on how it was functioning. On the other hand, if it were a project group meeting for a limited period to carry out some task, the group would be in a work mode if it not only pursued its task "effectively and single mindedly" (Bunker, 1974), but also set up structures to further the attainment of the work at hand.

In other words, during this mode, the group is experienced as flexible, able to live with ambiguity, and able to adapt and respond appropriately to the immediate. There is a healthy balance between task and maintenance roles, and the quality and amount of group productivity is viewed as the responsibility of the entire group. Here we see a group that is able to define its problems, test feasibility of suggested solutions, and confront issues that are undermining its functioning. An important feature of this mode is the singular absence of individual roles such as blocking, out-of-field behaviour, and digressing.

A cautionary note is raised by Rioch (1970) who suggests that groups which act **consistently** such as the ones described above, are rare, if non-existent in our society.

3.   Relationship between Work and Emotion

Work and emotional modes of group life are so interrelated that one never occurs without the other. At any given point, work and emotion may occur together in a number of different combinations, e.g., a group may be operating in a work dependency mode, a work pairing mode, or a work fight-flight mode. In other words, the work activity of a group is always influenced or associated with one or another of the above mentioned modes.

In a mature group however, the emotional modes while not necessarily resolved, are neither expressed nor focused on, but are channelled and redirected in such a way that they are integrated with the work level of the group. As a result of this kind of observation, Bion came to recognize that the work of a group is always influenced to some extent by certain emotional modes or concerns. Therefore, work occurs when the group **resists** the influence of one of these assumptions, and is able to apply on a consistent basis what it derives from experience.

4.   Valency Patterns

The concept of valency was introduced by Bion to describe an individual's **attraction** to a particular emotional mode. It is based on psychoanalytic theory which suggests that attitudes, values and habits developed in the first group in our lives, i.e., the family, influence our feelings and behaviour toward authority figures and toward other group members in later life.

In Bion's view everyone has some degree of valency with some individuals showing a propensity towards dependency, others towards fight-flight and still others towards pairing. These propensities explain why certain individuals become very active and verbal in a given situation, yet remain relatively silent and passive in others. The difference in responses (active versus passive) lies with the kind of valency to which individuals have the strongest tendency and the associated central assumption they subscribe to. Here, we also note how individuals with a given tendency instinctively move towards others with similar tendencies. This occurs spontaneously, and is done either to maintain the status quo, or to help move away from it.

The Relationship Between an Individual's Valence, Emotional Mode and Associated Assumptions

Emotional Mode	Valence	Assumptions
Dependency	Need for authority and structure	• I can't do it by myself. • I don't know enough. • I need someone stronger to rely on.
Counterdependency	Need for autonomy and freedom	• If I join them they may want something of me I can't deliver. • If I do it, this will cost me something. • If I show them I'm scared, I'll be taken advantage of.
Fight	Need for preservation	• Unless I fight, I will not get what I want. • If I don't do something about it now, I will lose my rights. • If I don't do something about this, it will become intolerable.
Flight	Need for protection	• If I ignore it, it will go away. • If I don't do it, someone else will. • It is easier to avoid certain difficulties and responsibilities than to face them.
Pairing	Need for intimacy	• I must be worthwhile if others like me. • If people show they like me, I'm part of things. • If I am close to others, this will bring me happiness.
Counterpairing	Need for integration of self	• If others get too close, I'll disappear. • If people get to know the real me, they won't like me. • If others get too close, I will be taken advantage of.

FIGURE I-6

Individuals who have a strong valency for dependency are more likely to rely on others for support and direction, wait for instruction rather than initiate action, and depend on others for their definition of success. On the other hand, individuals who have a strong valency for fight are more likely to confront, find fault, show feelings of dissatisfaction, express hostility freely, demand, bicker, nit-pick, etc. By the same token, individuals who have a strong valency for flight are more likely to ignore, by-pass, overlook, withdraw, minimize, or avoid facing important issues. Finally, those with a strong valency for pairing, are more likely to develop quick and easy group relations, invest energy into developing a warm and inclusive atmosphere in a group, and may express a desire to get close to others.

5.   The Individual and the Group

A central characteristic of Bion's theory of group development is his view of it as an entity. His framework suggests that the emotional modes and accompanying central assumptions are characteristics of the group as a whole, and not characteristic of the individual per se. This distinction is important to note, as students often tend to individualize these emotional cultures with statements such as "he is dependent," "she is in flight," etc. Thus, while the quality of the group emotion is frequently reflected in members' behaviours, Bion sees these behaviours as expressions of the group culture, with the individual merely "acting out" what exists in the group. In short, members act as "messengers of the culture" (Durkin, 1964).

What is not clear from Bion's work is how one determines the dominant group culture. Questions such as "how many group members must be involved before one can conclude it is the group speaking" begins to be important. Since the emotional mode refers to the entire group and since individual feelings are expressions of that mode, the question also arises, as to whether only one mode can exist at a given time. Answers to these questions are unclear. What is clear is that leaders using Bion's framework of how the group works, intervene with their group as an entity. Thus, while an intervention is frequently done through an individual, it is only because that individual represents what is going on in the group as a whole.

6.   Shifts in Emotional Modes

How do groups get stuck? How does one emotional mode give way to another, and how does a group shift to a work mode? Bion devotes particular attention to these questions.

First and foremost, it is important to understand that emotional modes do **not** get resolved in the true sense of the word, neither do they disappear, but are "used in the service of work task" (Rioch, 1970). The tension that is derived from the emotional modes gets transformed into group energy as the group gets confronted with its behaviour. The act which reveals the emotional mode results in giving way to a new emotional mode.

The confrontation brings about awareness which permits a restructuring of the collective tension into cohesive energy. This frees the group to either enter into a work mode, or shift into yet another emotional mode or preoccupation. It is this **recognition** of the group's individual freedom and this awareness of the binding tyranny of the emotional mode and its associated assumption that shifts the group out of its accumulated tension and converts it into building energy. Thus, when the group is not distracted it becomes "infused with direction" (Kellerman, 1981) and absorbed by its work.

A word about how groups get stuck and how they remain stuck. Bion notes that if members are deriving particular satisfaction from an emotional mode, the group is unlikely to shift out of that given mode, since no one is likely to be experiencing anxiety or tension. By the same token, if a group is preoccupied by an issue that generates an emotional mode, it cannot work effectively until it has transformed this anxiety into energy.

7.   Phases of Group Development

Bion did not imply any particular sequence to the order that the emotional modes appear, nor did he indicate that any one kind of basic assumption is more mature than another. However, his schema does seem to contain discernible phases and typical sequence of moods a group goes through.

Three phases seem to characterize this pendular model[1] of group development. In the first phase, group members are dependent on the leader; in the second phase, they begin to attack (fight) the leader, and/or run away (flight) from the leader. Next, they pass through a phase of pairing where they experience more intimate connections with each other. This is not a fixed sequence but varies with factors, such as the task demands of the group, and valence characteristics of its members.

To Bion, these phases are repetitive and recurring and vary in duration. Most often work appears in some combination an emotional mode, of which either work or emotion vary in being dominant at any given point. As the emotional modes change so does the image of authority.

8.   Group Formation

The overall growth of a group is affected by the composition of its members, its focus, and the method of its formation. Previous histories, compulsory attendance, performance expectations, group members' status, and work or social relations amongst members are some of the variables which influence the emotional modalities within a group.

---

[1] Pendular Model is one that stresses the shifts in boundaries of the group (Issacharoff, 1981).

For example, if a group is formed by members whose attendance is compulsory, then "fight" may be a common modality with disgruntled members, predisposed to resistance, confrontation and counterdependence. If the group is aware of the status hierarchy of its members, this could intensify the dependence modality with members tending to rely on others for support and direction. If on the other hand, the focus of the group is "how to build relationships" those with modalities associated with pairing may be common. By the same token, if the group is formed by members with a high preponderance for flight, then the tendency to ignore important issues would not be unusual.

A group with a wide range of valency types is more likely to deal with a wider range of emotional issues, than those with a narrow range. However, the likelihood of experiencing a preponderance of support, confrontation, withdrawal, etc., depends to a large extent on the valency composition within the group. Obviously, knowledge of a person's valence could be useful in determining which group they should join.

Bion's Framework for a Healthy Group

1. **A common purpose** towards which group members focus, whether it be defending, overcoming, creating or working on something.

2. **Common recognition** by group members of its "boundaries" and its relation and position in regards to other groups.

3. The ability to **absorb new members, and lose others** without fear of losing its identity

4. **Freedom from the tyranny of subgroups** that exclude or impose conditions on its members.

5. Members are **valued and free** to be themselves.

6. Group is able to **confront and cope with discomfort and discontent** within its ranks.

FIGURE I-7

PERSONAL NOTES ON BION

REFERENCES

Bennis, W. G. (1964). Patterns and vicissitudes in t-group development. In L. P. Bradford, J. R. Gibb, & K. D.

Benne (Eds.). *T-group theory and laboratory methods.* New York: John Wiley and Sons, Inc. 248-278.

Bion, W.R. (1961). *Experiences in groups.* New York: Ballantine.

Dimock, H. G. (1987). *Groups: Leadership and group development.* San Diego: University Associates, Inc.

Dunphey, D. G. (1968). Phases, roles and myths in self-analytic groups. *Journal of Applied Behavioural Science, 4,* 195-226.

Durkin, H. (1964). *The group in depth.* New York: International Universities Press Inc.

Gibb, J. R. (1964). Climate for trust formation. In L. P. Bradford, J. R. Gibb, & K.D. Benne (Eds). *T-group theory and laboratory methods.* New York: John Wiley and Sons, Inc. 279-309.

Golembiewski, R. T., & Blumberg, A. (1977). *Sensitivity training and the laboratory approach: Readings about concepts and applications.* New York: Peacock.

Hare, P. A. (1976). *Handbook of small group research* (2nd ed.). New York: Free Press.

Hare, P. A. (1982). *Creativity in small groups.* Beverley Hills: Sage Publications.

Issacharoff, A. (1981). The consequence of group cohesion & group death: The process of a time-limited group. In H. Kellerman (Ed.), *Group cohesion: Theoretical and clinical perspectives.* New York: Guine and Stratton.

Kark, R., Shamir, B., & Chen, G. (2003). The two faces of transformational leadership: Empowerment and dependency. *Journal of Applied Psychology, 88(2),* 246-255.

Kellerman, H. (1981). The deep structures of group cohesion. In H. Kellerman (Ed.), *Group cohesion: Theoretical and clinical perspectives.* New York: Guine and Stratton.

Luft, J. (1984). *Group process* (3rd ed.). California: Mayfield Publishing.

McLeish, J., Matheson, W., & Park, J. (1973). *The psychology of the learning group.* London: Hutchinson, University Library.

Mills, T. M. (1964). *Group transformation: An analysis of a learning group.* New Jersey: Prentice Hall.

Peck, S. (1987). *The different drummer.* London: Smith & Schuster Inc.

Rioch, M. J. (1970). *The work of Wilfred Bion on groups.* Psychiatry, 33, 56-66.

Rose, S. D. (1989). *Working with adults in groups.* London: Josey Bass.

Schutz, W. (1966). *Firo: A three dimensional theory of interpersonal behaviour. Reprinted as (1989). The interpersonal underworld.* Palo Alto, CA: Science and Behaviour Books; and Mill Valley, CA.: W. Schutz Associates.

Shaffer, J. B., & Galinsky, M. D. (1974). *Models of group therapy and sensitivity training.* New Jersey: Prentice Hall.

Shepherd, C. R. (1964). *Small groups: Some sociological perspectives.* San Francisco: Chandler Publications.

Smith, P. B. (1972) T-group training. In M.C. Berger, & P.J. Berger, (Ed). *Group training techniques.* Essex: Power Press.

Stock, D., & Thelen, H. A. (1958). *Emotional dynamics and group culture.* Washington, D.C.: National Training Laboratories.

Wheelan, S.A., Davidson, B., & Tilin, F. (2003). Group development across time - reality or illusion? *Small Group Research*, 34(2), 223-245.

Yalom, I. D. (1970). *The theory and practice of group psychotherapy.* New York: Basic Books.

II. GIBB'S TORI THEORY OF TRUST FORMATION

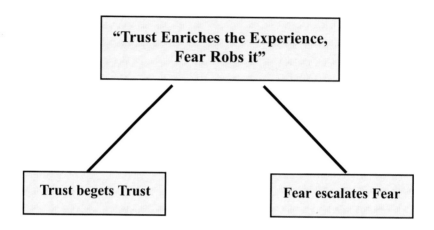

OVERVIEW

Gibb's (1978) TORI theory of personal, group and organizational development focuses on trust level as a primary determiner of group effectiveness and productivity. His theory clearly points to trust as the "pacemaker variable" in the growth of the group with fear being the single most crippling force working against this trust. He discusses his theory from a standpoint of growth and development and suggests that groups like people grow and that trust and fear are keys to understanding persons and social systems.

TORI theory suggests that fear is unresolved trust or mistrust and where trust is high relative to fear, people function well. Derived from the German word "Trost", meaning comfort, trust indicates an instinctive unquestioning belief in and reliance upon someone or something that will not fail in any situation where protection, discretion or fairness is essential. The word emphasizes this feeling of certainty whether it is justified or misguided. Gibb maintains that the presence or absence of this deep-seated conviction can make a powerful difference in our lives since trust provides an environment that nourishes personal growth while fear takes it away.

We know from Erikson's (1959) model of Developmental Tasks (key learnings for life survival) that the first psychosocial crisis faced by the developing individual is that of trust vs. mistrust. Similarly the first concern facing the individual in the group is trust vs. mistrust. The parent-child relationship lays the foundation for trust in oneself and in others, which is basic to personality development. However, this crisis also presents the challenge of mistrust in others, and a lack of confidence in oneself. This gets played out in the early stages of group life where individuals devise creative ways to cover up their fears and mistrust (Gibb, 1978).

In Gibb's theory trust and fear are antonyms representing polar ends of the central life process. Fear constrains and blocks whereas trust is a releasing process. In other words when I direct my energy to the fear, it cannot be utilized for growth. Fear reduction is the central dynamic of growth. Fears are self-fulfilling; they can only be reduced by sustained experience that invalidates them.

Gibb's is a growth oriented model where the development of the group is dependent on the growth of the individual and where "the person who dares to entrust him/herself to others goes far in creating a climate of trust in the group" (Egan, 1970). Since trust releases and fear constrains, a group is held back unless it develops trust. Gibb describes these two opposing forces this way:

> **Trust** creates the flow and gentles the mind-body-spirit. When I trust myself I am able to enter fully into the process of discovering and creating who I am. When I trust my own inner processes I am able to become what I am meant to become. When I trust you I am able to allow you in. And when I trust the processes of living, I am able to join others in the life journey.
>
> **Fear** stops the flow and arouses the defences. I direct my energies not into discovering and creating, but toward protecting myself from seen, expected or fantasized dangers. I am not sure of who I am; I cover up and put on protective masks, become concerned about how I ought to meet the expectations of others, and find it difficult to be with others. (Gibb, 1978, p.15).

TORI is an acronym for the four dimensions on which this theory is based: Trust "being who I am," Openness "showing who I am," Realization "doing what I want," and Interdependence "being with others." Arising out of these four dimensions are four modal concerns which are central to the formation of the group and which are processed throughout the life of the group. These modal concerns are Acceptance, Data Flow Goal Formation and Social Control.[1] They are similar to Schutz's "Interpersonal Need Areas" (Schutz, 1958) and are called "modal" in that Gibb believes that they are "universal" and represent commonly shared concerns basic to human growth needs. He sees these concerns arising from all social interaction and pervading all interpersonal relationships. They are focussed upon particularly in the T-Group process (Gibb, 1964).

Link Between the Individual and TORI Processes

Basic TORI Processes	Processes within the Person	Modal Concerns	Direction of Behavioural Growth
T - Trust	Being who I am	Acceptance	Impersonal to Personal
O - Openness	Showing who I am	Data Flow	Closed to Open
R - Realization	Doing what I want	Goal Formation	Imposed to Self-determining
I - Control	Being with others	Social Control	Dependence or Counter-dependence to Interdependence

Figure II-1
Adapted from the Annual Handbook of Group Facilitators, 1977.

---

[1] The term "Social Control" has been used throughout this chapter to differentiate between Schutz's Interpersonal Need Area of Control and Gibb's Modal Concern Area of Control. In Schutz's framework control refers to an individual's need to influence, dominate, take charge, be responsible and have authority over others. In Gibb's framework control has to do with group organizational structures that can be developed into "stable", "trust-able", "freedom-giving flexible forms" of interdependence and mutuality.

Acceptance:

This concern has to do with acceptance of self and others, the reduction of fears and gaining of membership in the group. Gibb sees this concern as one of the most crucial factors as unresolved acceptance cripples and paralyses the development and growth of the group.

Data Flow:

This concern has to do with opening valid information, the flow of spontaneous communication regarding how members feel, how they see things, what their attitudes are about the relevant concerns of the group, and the translation of this data into decision-making and choices.

Goal Formation:

This concern has to do with determining member wants, the integration of this data into group action plans and problem-solving with a goal of translating this process into productive and creative work.

Social Control:

This concern has to do with group organizational structures that can be developed into "stable." "trust-able," "freedom-giving flexible forms" of interdependence and mutuality.

These four modal concerns are interdependent and "continually recurring themes or processes of all groups." They flow together and build on each other. They are constantly reworked in the life of the group. They are perceived in the verbal and non-verbal behaviours of group members (Gibb, 1964). These concerns are so powerful that members instinctively attempt to reduce them. It is this movement towards reduction of these modal concerns that produces growth and development within the group. According to Gibb "life is the process of continual confrontation and resolution of these issues" with growth consisting of "increased resolution of these concerns" (Gibb, 1968). Thus the group becomes the confrontational ground for the individual.

Growth occurs concurrently on all four dimensions, but optimal growth occurs when "deepest and earliest" concerns arise in the following order: **acceptance**, **data flow**, **goal formation** and **social control**. For example we cannot trust others unless we trust and accept ourselves first. Data flow is only possible within the limits of trust formation. Setting realistic individual and group goals can only take place as "uncluttered and open" data is available, while a stable group structure (social control) is only possible through consensual goal setting.

Trust Assumptions

Self-acceptance is seen by Gibb as one of the most crucial factors in the development of the group as unresolved issues in this area cripples and paralyses its growth. This theory is based on the central assumption that we cannot trust others unless we trust and accept ourselves first. It is only with self-acceptance that one can make "trust assumptions" that influence and encourage trust formation and a supportive group climate. Low trust assumptions, on the other hand, contributes to the mistrust fear cycle and the development of a defensive climate. Thus the two sets of processes inherent in the TORI framework: trust formation or mistrust fear cycle, which go on in both the person's intrapersonal and interpersonal environment are put to the test.

Effects on the Group Under Conditions of Low Trust

	Acceptance	Data Flow	Goal Formation	Social Control
L o w T r u s t R e s o l u t i o n	Attempts made to change people's attitudes and beliefs.	Covering up of feelings, avoidance of the free flow of direct experience.	"Busy work" mistaken for creative and productive work.	Instance upon formal rules of debate and things kept at an impersonal basis.
	Members experience need for role definition and clarification.	Extremes in slow and rapid decision-making begin to emerge.	Energy diverted into meeting expectations of others. Work undertaken from a sense of duty with no interest.	Lines of authority are clearly drawn and role specifications formalized.
	Development of protective pairing, collusion and sub-grouping.	Withholding skills used.	Members move towards persuasion or attempts at changing others.	Development of persuasive methods of controlling and manipulating others and managing the process.
	Distortion of perception and suspicion about the motives of others.	Emergence of gossip, grapevine and washroom interchanges.	Difficulty in determining intrinsic motivation of group members.	Preoccupation with boundary setting and protecting one's turf.
	Resistance to initiation of action.	Group members hoard relevant feelings, opinions and perceptions.	Needs and desires of members are reflected in the activities of group.	Setting external rewards in the form of competition.
	Little or no risk- taking, facades, flattery and interpersonal formality.	Assumptions get turned into facts.	Apathy, boredom and competition prevail.	Advice-giving and power struggles.

FIGURE II-2

Effects on Group Behaviour Under Conditions of High Trust

	Acceptance	Data Flow	Goal Formation	Social Control
High Trust Resolution	Diversity becomes accepted and appreciated as potential strengths.	Focus directed to participation, consensual decision-making and choice.	Intrinsic goals of individuals integrated with goals of group.	Functional inter-dependence in role distribution and action planning.
	Members how vulnerability with minimal concern for danger or hurt.	Members freely and spontaneously express opinion and make it clear how they feel. Tolerance of deviations present.	Optimal number of members involved in different activities.	Marked inter-changeability of critical roles.
	Marked increase in confidence in group's work product.	People are heard and feedback is used to modify goals, decision-making and action plans.	Members know what they want and are aware they are doing what they desire.	Power structure becomes relatively open and participative.
	Members no longer need to stay in role and become personal and genuine.	Real problems and issues get dealt with openly and directly.	Work is purposeful and meaningful with members experiencing creativity and enthusiasm.	Optimal distribution of tasks which get allocated by interest and consensus with legitimate influence exerted.
	Members able to show inter-personal warmth.	Increased data available for problem-solving.	Marked increase in member involve-ment, loyalty and group strength.	Problem-solving arises spontaneously in response to needs.
	Group becomes open to emergent outcomes.	Conflict openly acknowledged and dealt with and seen	Conflict is minimal with emphasis on power and competition reduced.	Marked increase in interdependence and cooperation.

FIGURE II-3

35

"FEAR BEGETS FEAR"
Mistrust-Fear Cycle
Fear breeds fear - it constrains - it is self-fulfilling.

This section will deal briefly with the difficult and painful experience of what it is like to enter a group with a low trust level and a high fear/defence level. The context is that of a "Human Relations" group or a "Personal Growth" group. The description assumes that low trust assumptions contribute to the mistrust-fear cycle and the development of a defensive climate.

The following are some low-mistrust assumptions about self and others that influence a member's entry point in a group:

Low Trust Assumptions about Self	Low Trust Assumptions about Others
• I am not worth listening to • I am not O.K. if I fail • I am not a likeable and lovable person • I am not a worthwhile person • I am not a capable and competent person	• People are lazy • People cannot be trusted • People are externally motivated to set goals • People are irresponsible and require external rewards • People will take advantage of a supportive and trusting environment

FIGURE II-4

Since fear, according to Gibb, is the natural state at the onset of group formation and since members in a group are constantly influenced by two contrapuntal need systems[2], growth vs defence needs, these two opposing needs create tension and ambivalence within the individual. The tension stems from not knowing whether to respond to the fear component or the trust component. This mixture of hope and trepidation provide the ingredients for an initial climate of doubt and hesitation.

---

[2] **Contrapuntal needs** are opposite or contrary needs that create tension and ambivalence within the individual.

Here the member's lens of trust-mistrust blurs the capacity to comprehend what is going on and the fear gets camouflaged by a facade. Thus, like a child on the first day of school, it is not uncommon to "feel inadequate, but afraid to show it," or "feel tentative but need to appear certain." Moreover, instead of trusting the process of growth group members tend to try to "steer" it.

This mistrust not only exerts its force by manipulating the flow of conversation but also in controlling the behaviour and motivations of others. Therefore any "structures" or controls the group may impose on the individual not only increases the mistrust and confirms the underlying assumptions that people have about groups, but also lends "emotional support and strong motivation to continue the low-trust, high fear behaviour" (Gibb, 1965).

While defences help us in life, they also may prevent us from capitalizing on learning situations. The fear that the individual feels, "leads to caution, to holding back and to the filtering" (Gibb, 1978). Thus, data flow becomes "distorted" and "restricted." This manipulation of the communication flow coupled with "attempts to change attitudes and beliefs of others" and attempts to "make decisions for others" lead to inappropriate assumptions, such as "silence means consent." Thus the problem of data processing influences the problem of decision making and choice which in turn influences the surfacing or identifying of the intrinsic motivation of group members. Under such defensive conditions the group develops methods of controlling and manipulating others while others in turn become preoccupied with boundary setting and protecting their "turf."

An interactive and negative self-preserving cycle is thus set in motion. The greater the fear and distrust, the greater the "circumvention counter-strategy and counter-distortion" is experienced. Thus the clear feedback so necessary to the system gets denied. Bateson (1979) observes that it is "only through negative feedback that knowledge develops for it provides a contrast" while Smith and Berg (1987) suggest that "it is out of the information created from the distinctions between the positive and the negative, that the capacity of the system to reflect is created."

"TRUST BEGETS TRUST"
Trust Formation Cycle
It is only through trust that trust can be built.

This section will deal briefly with the rich and precious experience of what it is like to enter a group with a high trust level and a low fear/defence level. Similar to the previous section, the context is that of a "Human Relations" group or a "Personal Growth" group. The description assumes that high trust assumptions contribute to the acceptance of self and others and the development of a supportive climate.

The following are some high pre-trust assumptions about self and others that influence a member's entry point in a group:

High Trust Assumptions about Self	High Trust Assumptions about Others
• I am worth listening to • I am O.K. if I fail • I am a likeable and lovable person • I am a worthwhile person • I am a capable and competent person	• People are trustworthy • People can be trusted • People are internally motivated to set goals • People are responsible, loyal and appropriately work-oriented • People learn and grow in a supportive environment.

FIGURE II-5

While the fear mentioned in the previous section is still the natural state at the onset of group formation, it is experienced quite differently by the person with trust assumptions. He/she is more likely to be the one to take a risk even if the climate of psychological safety may not be in evidence at the time. It is this person "who dares to entrust himself to others" that "goes far in creating a climate of trust in the group" (Egan, 1970). Gibb observes this about such a person stating that "one who freely shares data, whether of feelings or figures reduces fear and distrust in himself and in others."

According to Gibb (1964), groups "with high acceptance of self and others show a reduction of fear and distrust." There is a maximum flow of free and open communication where feedback serves to "modify goal formation and decision-making" and where activities get related to goals which are "explicit and verbalized."

Within this particular structure there is a "reduction in humour and an increase in warmth." Diversity becomes accepted, members freely and spontaneously express opinions with increased data available for problem-solving. While conflict is openly acknowledged and dealt with, its occurrence is minimal. There is a marked increase in member involvement, confidence in the group's productivity and optimal distribution of member task roles. Problem-solving arises spontaneously in response to needs; interdependence and cooperation are in evidence.

Summary Overview of GIBB'S TORI Theory of Trust Formation

Modal Concern	Group Issue	Behaviours	Low Resolution of Concern	High Resolution of Concern	Early Development	Later Development
Trusting-Being • Acceptance • Warming	• Acceptance • Membership	• Accepting self/others • Trusting • Experiencing warmth • Seeing differences	• Facades • Avoidance of conflicts/feelings • Cynicism • Flattery	• Reduction in mistrust • Increase in warmth • Confidence in group • Deviations accepted	• Need for status • Fear of inadequacy • Conformity • Need for role definition	• Trust/Risking "my space is fine" • Feelings of adequacy • Diversity welcomed
Opening-Showing • Letting in • Joining • Listening • Empathizing	• Data flow • Decision-making • Choices	• Spontaneity • Rapport • Depth of communication • Disclosing	• Denial of feelings • Artificial politeness • Showing great concern over hurting another's feelings • "Weather talk"	• Frequent use of feedback • Conflict recognized, dealt with, and used creatively • Decisions verified, consensus or near consensus	• Ambiguity • Gimmicks • Caution in risk-taking • Distortion	• Clear, direct • Spontaneous expressions • Sharing • Impulsive expression

FIGURE II-6a

Summary Overview of GIBB'S TORI Theory of Trust Formation (cont'd)

Modal Concern	Group Issue	Behaviours	Low Resolution of Concern	High Resolution of Concern	Early Development	Later Development
Realizing-Achieving • Asserting • Exploring • Evolving • Wanting	• Control • Organization Motivation & Needs **Into** Actions & Sequences	• Facades • Avoidance of conflicts/feelings • Cooperating • Giving and getting freedom	• Coercive or persuasion methods of exerting influence • Apathy • Passive resistance to productivity • Whispering, irrelevant debates, semantic quibbling	• Personal goals into group goals • Goals are explicit and verbalized • Goals change as task is completed • Optimal involvement	• Persuasive advice • Competition • Rivalry • Apathy • Diffuse goals • Withdrawal	• Involvement • Cooperative behaviour • Creativity • Clarity of goals • Enthusiasm
Interdependency-Inter-Being • Integrating • Joining • Sharing • Synergizing	• Control • Organizing	• Participating • Cooperating • Giving and getting freedom	• Advice giving • Debate • Argument • Power struggles • Abdication of responsibility	A group that is: • Open • Manageable • Flexible • Spontaneous • Easily modified • Optimum ability to inter-change critical roles	• Structure • Channels • Rules • Focus • Concern for leadership • Dependency • Bargaining	• Informality • Anarchy • No need for rules • Little need for leader • Flexibility

FIGURE II-6b
Adapted from Gibb, 1978.

KEY FEATURES OF GIBB'S THEORY

1. **Not a stage theory**

2. **Rhythm and movement of change**

3. **No termination stage**

4. **Contrapuntal need system**

5. **Mistrust-fear cycle**

6. **Primacy and paradox of trust**

7. **Growth of group dependent on growth of individual**

1.   Not a Stage Theory

This is not a stage theory but a growth directed humanistic one with an optimal sequence in the development of the four modal concerns. The tendency to assume that each of these concerns represents a particular stage in the group's development is quite common i.e. acceptance being the first stage and social control the last issue. This is not so. While acceptance and trust formation are a prerequisite to the development of the other three factors these modal concerns are neither stages nor phases of group development but central concerns that groups wrestle with as group formation takes place. While each concern has a developmental component to it (unresolved - resolved), "these four factors are processed throughout the life of the group and continually flow together and build on each other" (Dimock, 1987, p.76). As these represent life issues they are never resolved completely. Any reference to early or later growth development is in connection with the resolution of "intertwined" themes and sub-themes arising in the four modal concerns and not the stage development of a particular modal concern. In other words a group can be at a later point of group development (time span a group has been together), but still dealing with an earlier growth concern in its resolution of trust and fear reduction.

Key Behaviours Expressed in Group Development

Modal Concern	From Early Development	To Later Development
Acceptance This modal concern has to do with the formation of trust, membership and the acceptance of self and others.	Fear Observing Suspicion Rigidity Conformity	Trust Engaging Confidence Flexibility Diversity
Data Flow This modal concern has to do with communication, decision-making and feedback.	Withholding Strategy Distortion Secrecy Censoring	Disclosing Spontaneity Clarity Truth Transparency
Goal Formation This modal concern has to do with teamwork, productivity and intrinsic motivation of members.	Persuasion Conformity Passivity Competition	Participation Creativity Enthusiasm Collaboration
Social Control This modal concern has to do with coordination, procedures and distribution of member role.	Dependent Domination Conformity Rigidity Outer-directedness	Interdependency Cooperation Adaptablity Flexibility Inner-directedness

FIGURE II-7

2. Rhythm and Movement of Change

To say there are no changes of group development is not to say that there are no changes in the group's development over time. Changes do occur but the process of group formation and group growth is unpredictable. Each group's development is influenced by its own set of circumstances and therefore moves at its own pace. Research indicates that in some groups "change seems to proceed in dramatic and unpredictable spurts" and in others "long periods pass with either regressive movement or plateaus of no progress, with occasional dramatic spurts at the end" (Gibb, 1964).

While the optimal sequence of change in the TORI framework is sequential (i.e., acceptance - data flow - goal formation - social control) it does not preclude change in a cyclical or spiral form with movement back and forth across dimensions. Trust however is the "pacemaker" for it is upon the development of this particular dimension that the other three depend.

In other words, each factor in this contingency hierarchy provides a pace-setting for the factors lower in the hierarchy. Thus openness is contingent on trust development, quality problem-solving on access to a functional communication system and optimal distribution of member roles on commitment and interest to the activity at hand. Hence, while there is an optimal sequence in the development of these modal concerns, movement on all four concerns occurs concurrently and interdependently.

3. No Termination Stage

This is an open-ended theory where trust building is seen as a never ending process and where the four modal concerns are seen as "Universal Life Issues" that never fully reach completion. Thus the usual termination stage often referred to in other theories of group development does not apply here. For example, Lacoursiere's (1980) Life Cycle of Groups five stage theory begins with "Orientation" and ends with "Termination" and Tuckman's (1965) Developmental Sequence in Small Groups four stage theory begins with "Formation" and ends with "Adjournment." On the other hand Schutz's (1966) Three Dimensional Theory of Interpersonal and Group Behaviour more closely resembles Gibb's TORI framework where the usual termination stage does not apply. Schutz's theory, like Gibb's, represents three basic human growth needs (inclusion-control-openness) that are never ending and which get recycled and reworked throughout the life of the group.

4. Contrapuntal Need System

Members in a group are constantly influenced by two contrapuntal need systems - growth needs vs. defence needs. These opposite or contrary needs create tension and ambivalence within the individual. The tension stems from not knowing whether to respond to the fear component or the trust component. Hence, the prevalence of apparent paradoxical behaviour seen in groups i.e. "…some withdrawal in approach, some hostility in affection, some manipulation in sharing and some deception in openness" (Gibb, 1968).

Gibb sees growth as a constant process of counterbalancing these needs within the individual. He also sees the group as serving an arena in which the tensions between the defence and the need to know get played out.

This counterbalancing of the contrapuntal need system is what gives Gibb's theory the constant ebb and flow and up and down movement in the hierarchy. It also explains the constant reworking and revisiting of these modal concerns. Thus when a concern is said to have been resolved it does not mean it has been completed and terminated. What it does mean is that the tension associated around this concern has been reduced. In other words, growth within the TORI framework consists of continual confrontation of fear and resolution of the fear-induced anxiety.

5. Mistrust-Fear Cycle

The mistrust-fear cycle experienced by so many in a group is unintentional. The individual does not enter a group with the intention of deliberately engaging in this cycle. Yet the experience of entering a new group seems to confirm the individual's underlying low trust assumptions he/she may have about people and groups. This fear, in turn, activates a self-preservation cycle, which in turn encourages the individual to use facades or communication distortions for protection and self-preservation. Since "fear breeds fear" and since it is only through "trust that trust can be built" the continuing mistrust-fear cycle gets reinforced as "trust depends on itself to get started" (Gibb, 1965). What becomes clear is that for trust to grow and develop members must trust the group and the group must trust its members.

Contrapuntal Need System in the Person

Basic Modal Concern	From Early Development	To Later Development
Acceptance	**Love:** To give and receive love, trust, warmth and acceptance.	**Punishment:** To give and receive punishment and derision; to manage and manipulate warmth.
Data Flow	**Intimacy:** To give and receive openness, straightforward communication, genuineness, and depth.	**Distance:** To give and receive social distance, to withdraw and to influence intimacy.
Goal Formation	**Realization:** To give and receive personal inner satisfaction, motivation and self-determination of goals.	**Persuasion:** To give and receive persuasion, imposition, manipulation and to strategize goals.
Social Control	**Freedom:** To give and receive interdependence flexibility and freedom.	**Control:** To give and receive tight controls and sanctions, to be dominant, demanding, dependent or aggressively independent.

FIGURE II-8
Adapted from Gibb, 1968.

6. Primary and Paradox of Trust

The central role that trust plays in Gibb's theory cannot be underscored sufficiently. Gibb claims that trust is absolutely essential for growth to take place and that little if anything can happen in a group until members learn to trust one another.

Research focusing directly on Gibb's model of trust formation reveals that pre-laboratory trust is a key predicator of eventual group accomplishment (Friedlander, 1971). In other words the trust level assumptions a member brings into a group is critical to the group's development.

Since many of us fail to grow because we insist on having a climate of absolute safety before we venture to take a risk and, since fear is the natural state at the onset of group formation, the person with trust assumptions is more likely to be the one to take a risk even if the a climate of psychological safety may not be in evidence at the time. It is this person "who dares to entrust himself to others" that "goes far in creating a climate of trust in the group" (Egan, 1970).

Breaking out of the bonds of mistrust is not easy particularly since it is "only through trusting that trust is built". Smith and Berg (1987) in their study on group dynamics examine the paradoxical epistemology of trust pointing out that, in order for trust to develop, it must depend on itself to get started.

7. Growth of the Group Dependent on Growth of the Individual

In the TORI framework, the influence of the individual's trust orientation is key to the group's growth. The individual's prehistory to the group and their pre-trust assumptions become a critical dynamic. As the individual moves from reduction of fear and resolution of anxiety, formation of trust begins to take place. Growth is a directional movement - one contributes to one's own growth and the growth of others. Thus growth is reciprocal. For Gibb, this reciprocity and direction is "toward trust and personal relationships and away from fear and impersonal relationships" (Gibb, 1968). However, it is "the process of trusting rather than the content of the trust that strengthens the relationships within the group," which in turn makes them feel "trustable" (Smith and Berg, 1987). Group members are usually ready to respond and engage in kind. The interactive process in turn influences the growth of the group as it begins to experience the rich outcomes of the cumulative reduction of fear and the concomitant resolution of trust. A paradigm shift of growth and development ensues. However, to be truly effective growth must occur for all individuals involved. If one person in the group fails to develop trust, then the growth relationship is not truly effective.

How to Reduce Fear

While no one can program the development of trust in a group, much can be done to facilitate its development. It is with this in mind using Gibb's framework as a background that the following suggestions have been made.

Create and Communicate a Safe Atmosphere	Climate of psychological safety must not only exist but must also be communicated to the group if it is to have any influence on the group's interpersonal behaviour.
Encourage Members to Voice their Fears	The importance of public expression of fears cannot be underscored enough. Fears that are recognized, 'owned' and shared with others become more acceptable and easier to deal with.
Help Members Recognize that they are Not Alone	The healing process involved in recognizing the similarities is particularly useful at the onset of a group when the natural state is that of mistrust and fear.
Encourage the Development of Maintenance Roles	The development of maintenance roles is often neglected in a group. Its development helps members narrow the gap between what is expressed and what is wanted.
Nurture the Development of Spontaneity	This is a precious and central feature of the TORI framework, for spontaneity seems to be the channel through which individuals are able to learn from the inside out.

FIGURE II-9

48

SUMMARY STATEMENT

Gibb is a powerful theory of group development for it bears great relevance to concepts related to experiential learning, responsibility taking and relationship building. As a professor teaching in a department that espouses a philosophy of learning by doing, this theory has influenced the design of my courses and the diagnosis of problems that have arisen in my classroom. It has also helped me recognize that the times I have not paid attention to the development of trust within the classroom have not been without paying a heavy toll - a toll on the student's development, a toll on the subject matter at hand and a toll on the potential development of a co-learning relationship between my myself and my students.

PERSONAL NOTES ON GIBB

REFERENCES

Bateson, G. (1979). *Mind and Culture.* New York: Bantam.

Corey, M.S. & Crogan, G. (1992). *Groups: Process and Practice,* (4th ed.). CA: Brooks/Cole Publishing Co.

Cragan, J.F. & Wright, D.W. (1995). *Communicating in small groups.* Boston: Wadsworth Publishing Co.

Dimock, H.G. (1987). *Groups: Leadership and group development.* San Diego: University Associates, Inc.

Egan, G. (1970). *Encounter: Group Processes for interpersonal growth.* Belmont, CA: Brooks/Cole Publishing Co.

Forsyth, D.R. (1999). *Group dynamics* (3rd ed.). Boston: Wadsworth Publishing Inc.

Friedlander, F. (1971). The primacy of trust as a facilitator of further group accomplishment. In C.L. Cooper & L.L. Maugham (Eds), T-Groups: *A survey of research.* Toronto: Wiley Interscience.

Gibb, J.R. & Gibb, L.M. (1978). The group as a growing organism. In L.P. Bradford (Ed.), *Group Development.* City, CA: University Associates, 1978.

Gibb, J.R. (1978). *Trust: A new view of personality and organizational development.* Los Angeles: The Guild of Tutors Press.

Gibb, J.R. (1972a). Managing for creativity in organizations. In *Climate for Creativity* (Ed.) C.W. Taylor. New York: Pergamon.

Gibb, J.R. (1972b). The search for with-ness: A new look at interdependence. In G.W. Dyer (Ed.), *Modern Theory and Method of Group Training.* New York: Van Nostrand.

Gibb, J.R. & Gibb, L.M. (1968). Leaderless groups: Growth-centered values and potentials. In H.A. Otto & J. Mann (Eds), *Ways of Growth.* New York: Grossman.

Gibb, J.R. (1968a). The Counselor as a role-free person. In C. Parker (Ed.), *Science and Human Affairs.* Palo Alto: Science and Behavior Books.

Gibb, J.R. (1968b). Humanistic elements in group growth. In J.F.T. Bugental (Ed.), *Challenges of humanistic psychology.* New York: McGraw Hill.

Gibb, J.R. (1965). Fear and facade: Defensive management. In R.E. Farson (Ed.), *Science & Human Affairs.* Palo Alto: Science and Behaviour Books.

Gibb, J.R. (1964). Climate for trust formation. In L.P. Bradford, J.R. Gibb & K.D. Benne (Eds.), *T-group theory and laboratory methods.* New York: Wiley and Sons Ltd.

Golembiewski, R.T. & Blumberg, A. (1977). *Sensitivity training and the laboratory approach: Readings about concepts and applications.* New York: Peacock.

Hare, Paul A. (1976). *Handbook of small group research.* New York: Free Press.

Kass, R. (1983). *The apology stance in the learning process.* Unpublished doctoral dissertation, University of Toronto.

Lacoursiere, R. (1980) *The life cycle of groups: Group development stage theory.* New York: Human Sciences Press.

Schutz, W.C. (1966). FIRO - *A three dimensional theory of behaviour.* Reprinted as *The interpersonal underworld.* Palo Alto, CA: Science and Behavior Books.

Smith, K. & Berg, D.N. (1987). A paradoxical conception of group dynamics. *Journal of Human Relations,* 40, 633-658. .

Tuckman, B.W. (1965). Developmental sequence in small groups. *Psychological Bulletin, 63,* (6), 384-39.

III. LACOURSIERE'S LIFE CYCLE OF GROUPS

OVERVIEW

This developmental stage theory was developed in 1980 by Roy Lacoursiere who is a psychiatrist at the Menninger School of Psychiatry, Topeka, Kansas. His work is based on a thorough review of existing literature and research data on group development. Using his empirical findings, he put together his life cycle model of groups. His data base includes studies on training, psychotherapy and encounter groups, task, problem-solving and learning groups, committees, and work teams. He excluded single group studies, and most open-ended groups. The groups he reviewed varied in size, composition, length of meetings, and number of meetings.

The model he presents is a five stage progressive model of group development. The stages are: **orientation, dissatisfaction, resolution, production,** and **termination**. They are named according to the predominant theme they represent. These stages occur in a regular sequence and while they overlap and blend one into another, they are quite separate and distinct. This does not mean that once a stage is passed, issues central to that stage do not reappear. On the contrary, traces of earlier stages can be seen in later ones and vice versa. For example, aspects of orientation are dealt with throughout the life of the group and feelings of dissatisfaction are not isolated to just one stage. The length of stages in this model varies according to type and focus, its clarity and the ease with which it can be completed.

Each stage includes task and socio-emotional behaviour. Task behaviours are functions of defining, testing feasibility of suggestions and ideas, learning and applying of skills related to the task, assessing what needs to be achieved, and determining how to achieve it. Socio-emotional behaviours are related to reactions, feelings and interaction of group members toward the task, the leader and other members.

In groups where the focus is less personal e.g., work groups and committees, task and socio-emotional behaviours are quite separate and easily distinguishable. Whereas in groups where the focus is personal and interactive, e.g., therapy and training groups, task and socio-emotional behaviours are inseparable and more difficult to isolate. Fluctuations and shifts in the socio-emotional tone of the group are presented in terms of a "morale curve" (Dies, 1984).

Lacoursiere sees his life cycle model of groups as having universal application. Particularly as he sees few people, or groups, as being "free of experiences governed by these developmental stages and the associated changes in morale." This sequence is most conspicuous in groups that are of longer duration, in which membership is stable and where the task is personal and ego involving. When the group is of shorter duration, open-ended and where the task is impersonal and concrete, the sequence is "masked or distorted" (Hill & Gruner, 1973).

SUMMARY OVERVIEW OF LACOURSIERE'S LIFE CYCLE MODEL

Group Development Stage	Key Features
Orientation	Positive and unrealistic expectations.
Dissatisfaction	Encounter with the limitations of the experience.
Resolution	Reconciliation between reality and expectations.
Production	Commitment to constructive work.
Termination	Assessment and realistic appraisal of task.

FIGURE 111-1

ORIENTATION

Key Features

- **Positive and unrealistic expectations**

- **Inquiry and exchange of information**

- **Definition of the task**

- **Dependence on leader or situation**

This initial stage of group development is particularly important, as it is here that participants first get informed and oriented to the group, its members and its leader. This is a stage of getting acquainted, forming membership, and getting one's bearings. It is also a time of defining the task and what needs to be achieved. Lacoursiere suggests that most people, other than those forced to participate[3] enter new group experiences with enthusiasm, positive expectations, and optimism. While there is some preoccupation and anxiety about this new situation, hopes far outweigh disquieting thoughts and anticipatory fears that participants may have about concerns such as: the task, membership within the group, or its leadership. This positive orientation is not to be confused with the "honeymoon period syndrome" which is superficial and short-lived, often covering up resistance, opposition and negative orientation.

During this initial period there is heavy reliance on the group leader for guidance, content, and structure e.g. defining the common task, establishing boundaries, etc. This is a healthy dependence, for it propels participants to ask for ground rules and gives rise to group norms (Karterud & Foss, 1989). Roles appearing during this stage are predominately that of giving and seeking information, giving and seeking opinions and defining the task. While testing feasibility of what is required is visible, this is done minimally. Any maintenance roles such as coordinating, orienting, and facilitating, etc., appearing during this stage, are generally taken on by the leader.

---

[3] For elaboration on this concept, see section on **Negative Orientation** (p. 76).

Depending on the focus of the group (e.g., training vs. task groups) this initial stage of orientation can be quite short (less than 1 session) or quite protracted (more than 1/3 of the group's life). For example, in therapy and training groups where task and socio-emotional areas of behaviour are hard to separate and define, and skills arduous to acquire, clarification and exploration of what needs to be achieved consumes a major part of the group's effort and time. Hence, orientation in this case, not only extends over a long period of time, but also blends into subsequent stages, with traces of orientation still appearing in the resolution and productivity stages.

Concomitantly, orientation is quite short in task, work groups, in committees and in short-term problem solving groups, if the task and socio-emotional areas of behaviour are distinct and separate. It is also of a short duration if the task is impersonal and easy to define, and if relationships are habitual and familiar. In these particular instances, orientation consumes only a small fraction of the group's time. Thus, the time frame within this stage is flexible, with orientation expanding or contracting, depending on the task needed to be achieved.

While the degree of work achieved during the orientation stage is medium to moderate, a fair amount of energy is spent on defining the problem such as: "What is the task? How will we approach it? What skills do we need in order to accomplish it? What information do we need in order to proceed?"

Summary of Shifts in Morale, Work Level and Roles during the Orientation Stage

Group Development Stage	Morale	Work Level	Task Roles	Maintenance Roles	Individual Roles (Non-Functional)
Orientation	High or positive morale	Medium High focus on defining what needs to be done	Defining the task Giving and seeking information Giving and seeking opinions Some testing of feasibility	Rarely any in evidence	Rarely any in evidence

FIGURE III-2

58

DISSATISFACTION

Key Features

- **Encounters with the limitations of the experience**

- **Disequilibrium**

- **Decrease in self-esteem**

- **Frustration against task and authority figures**

This is a difficult stage characterized by frustration, ambiguity, and anxiety. Following the high hopes and positive expectations experienced in the orientation stage, reality sets in as the group begins to face the task at hand, as it examines what needs to be done and how to do it.

This "encounter with reality" is generally not only unpleasant, but also experienced as a bit of a shock. This unexpected encounter brings into sharp focus discrepancies between expectation and experience. Despite the fact that reality rarely lives up to a person's expectation, each time this is confronted, it is unexpected and has a jarring impact - almost like a staggering blow.

As the group examines what needs to be done, reality begins to conflict with the ideal. Frustration and anger set in as members begin to realize that they may not be able to accomplish what they had hoped, as they discover that they may not achieve the task as easily as had been expected, or that the initial reason why they joined the group was not what it seemed to be.

The anger expressed is a direct reaction to the frustration experienced. This is directed toward the authority figure, some aspect of the task, the group situation, other members, or even the individual herself/himself e.g., "I must be stupid." The response varies, depending on the focus of the group. In therapy or training groups, where the task has an interpersonal nature and where the group is more likely to get stuck, anger is usually directed toward both the authority figure and other group members. On the other hand, in task, work groups, committees, learning groups, and short-term problem-solving groups, anger is generally directed only toward the authority figure, particularly if the task is too vague and unrealistic, or when recommendations remain unheeded.

Feelings generated during the encounter with reality are: disappointment, resentment, discouragement, sadness, doubt, resistance, anxiety, anger, confusion, disequilibrium, disgruntlement, fear, crisis of confidence, etc. Morale[4] drops and hits its lowest point, work level becomes low to non-productive and enthusiasm wanes.

As these negative feelings prevail, they begin to dominate and far outweigh the more positive ones experienced during the earlier stage. Behaviours begin to match the feelings experienced with some of the more common ones being: members start coming in later and later, absenteeism begins to be regular and frequent, drop out starts occurring, stalling of work that needs to be accomplished is in evidence, and premature closure of the group is not uncommon, etc.

The group can get arrested at this stage. If this happens, demoralization sets in with the work of the group is negatively affected. This is particularly obvious in therapeutic settings with open-ended involuntary groups whose membership is either coerced or compulsory, and where the group never reaches or "reaches and then retreats" from the resolution.

Lacoursiere suggests that the intensity of dissatisfaction during this stage is in direct proportion to the "discrepancy between the reality of the situation and the expectations regarding the task." The longer the gap between the internal expectation and the reality of the situation, the greater the disappointment. The question arises as to what this internal expectation is based on, that the reality does not measure up to. For some, it might be the comparison of other group experiences. For others, the desire for the idealized family group that would provide what one had before or never had. For still others, it might represent hopes for a better experience than the last time, or the reward of certain kinds of knowledge and skill worth working for. For some, it might also represent the opportunity to contribute or excel in a certain area, etc.

While the intensity of this stage is related to the extent of incongruity between fact and fiction, environmental influences, member characteristics, nature of the work, prior relationships within the group, and willingness to adapt to the realities of the situation determine its length. While it has been suggested that the dissatisfaction stage comprises about 15% of the group's life, I believe that this is highly under-rated. I estimate that dissatisfaction sometimes lasts 40 or 50% or more of the group's life. In fact, sad as it might seem, often the largest segment of life in a group can be quite unpleasant.

Roles taken on during this stage shift to that of blocking, digressing and out-of-field. While some task roles continue to emerge such as giving opinions and testing feasibility, the earlier predominance of task roles seen in the orientation stage, wanes. Once again, maintenance roles continue to be taken on by the leader.

---

[4] For elaboration on this concept, see section on **Morale** (p. 78).

The group's progress into the resolution stage, depends largely on how the dissatisfaction stage has been handled. These two stages are closely connected in so far as the very process in which the group engages, in an attempt to resolve its reality discrepancies, suggesting that the group has in fact begun to enter the realm of resolution.

Dissatisfaction is inevitable! If orientation is solid, it does not mean that the group passes over this stage, although it might alter its length. No matter how well orientation has been handled and regardless of how realistically it has been dealt with, the realities of the situation are never clearer and more obvious to the group as in the dissatisfaction stage.

Summary of Shifts in Morale, Work Level and Roles during the Dissatisfaction Stage

Group Development Stage	Morale	Work Level	Task Roles	Maintenance Roles	Individual Roles (Non-Functional)
Dissatisfaction	Low Morale Here it hits its lowest point	Low to medium Non-productive stage as reality sets in	Giving opinions Testing feasibility	None in evidence	Blocking Digressing Out-of-field

FIGURE III-3

RESOLUTION

Key Features

- **Reconciliation between reality and expectations**

- **Setting boundaries**

- **Development of cohesion and group oriented norms**

- **Skills learned and applied in the immediacy**

This resolution stage, that falls between dissatisfaction and production, is an important one. For it is here that significant building blocks are laid, which influence depth, quality and success in the production stage.

What are these building blocks? How and why do they influence the production stage? Essentially what happens in this stage is a reconciliation between reality and expectations with members "encouraged to challenge the problem rather than challenge the group by acting out or dropping out" (Ettin, Heiman, & Kopel, 1988). Here the group examines its goals in the light of time available, the task it has to accomplish, the restrictions of the situation, and the skills accessible within the group. This leads into redefinition and clarification of what needs to be done, assessment of priorities, and needs analysis. Essentially, it means contracting to continue to work as a group.

This process of open discussion, ownership of dissatisfaction and willingness to compromise on the part of the group, sets the tone for cohesion building, thus, influencing a climate that favours effective group work. It also builds the platform for norm setting. For example, as cooperation amongst members begins to take place, the importance of maintenance roles begins to be clear. This is particularly obvious in therapy and training groups. If the process used by the group has matched its individual needs, the norms emerging out of it are usually constructive and useful.

Where the dissatisfaction has been unusually negative, severe or disruptive, this resolution process can take a long time since the concerns within the group need to be addressed and issues need to be worked through. In task groups, work groups, committees, short term problem-solving groups, and learning groups, this process is sometimes rushed and skipped over, with the group settling for a "hasty superficial band aid" in service of the task that needs to be accomplished. Here, time pressure exerts an influence on what needs to be accomplished, particularly if the group is working under a deadline.

As the group begins to set its method of working together and as structure and procedures are sorted through and decided upon, resources begin to be used and pooled, and skills begin to be learned with a forum for applying them provided in the immediacy of the "here and now." We note the lowering of tensions, decrease in dissatisfaction, increase in self-esteem, acceptance of differences, and lessening of anxiety as clarity overshadows the earlier ambiguity.

The duration of this stage varies with focus, extent to which expectations vary with the realities of the task, level of dissatisfaction and ease with which it is resolved and quality of the relationships within the group. As this stage evolves, the roles taken on by group members begin to balance between task and maintenance ones. We see task roles such as defining the problem, giving and seeking opinions, and information. The testing of feasibility that occurs has a different tone from that which appeared in the dissatisfaction stage. It is less of defiance and more of checking for reality and practicality. In the maintenance area we see roles such as coordinating, supporting, encouraging, and following. While individual roles (non-functional) still appear, they are in much less evidence than in the dissatisfaction stage. Work level rises and morale begins to climb. When negative feelings remain unresolved, morale remains low or dips further with demoralization setting in.

The resolution stage starts with a decrease in dissatisfaction and ends when there is an increase in work on the task accompanied by visibly discernible positive feelings.

Summary of Shifts in Morale, Work Level and
Roles during the Resolution Stage

Group Development Stage	Morale	Work Level	Task Roles	Maintenance Roles	Individual Roles (Non-Functional)
Resolution	Morale begins to climb	Medium to high Focus on task clarification and goal orientation	Defining the problem Giving and seeking information and testing feasibility	Coordinating Supporting-encouraging Following	Blocking Digressing Out-of-field All of the above, but much less in evidence

FIGURE III-4

PRODUCTION

Key Features

> - **Commitment to constructive work**
>
> - **Gain in insight and understanding**
>
> - **Mastery of skills**
>
> - **Increase in self-esteem**

This is the most productive stage in the group's life cycle. Attention is focused on the task with renewed anticipation, high hopes, and positive feelings of eagerness to be part of the experience.

Depending on the focus of the group, the process experienced by members varies. In task, work groups, committees and short term problem-solving teams, as the group settles down to work, a seriousness descends upon the team. The interaction is high, ideas flow and are exchanged easily, resources within the group become more evident, and skills hitherto undetected begin to surface. Healthy competition between members is seen but this does not get in the way of cooperation. At times, there is a need for further re-clarification of the task and modification of goals, but this is done in a spirit of openness and a desire to work more effectively. Time is used efficiently and most members show a willingness to take on responsibility for various tasks arising from the main task. The group can get bogged down as enthusiastic members driven by a desire to produce begin to over-extend themselves. Fatigue can set in and morale can drop. By and large however, this is a useful and productive time.

In learning groups, while there is a similar process to that of task groups, there is a subtle difference between work groups, committees, and short term problem-solving groups. Since "learning" is at the core, and since the group life is usually short term, some of its concrete immediate results may be less evident as the process of learning continues to take place well after the group's closure takes place. The group generally spends most of its time in this stage. Usually, interest to proceed with the task is high as outcomes are more closely related to members' interests and rationale for being there in the first place.

In therapy or training groups, the process is quite different. The earlier dissatisfaction and tension, which had lowered in the resolution phase, begins to dissipate visibly as members begin to experience new learnings, new skills, and opportunities to apply and practice them. The very process of acquiring new skills raises positive feelings that influence self-esteem. The process also generates feelings of adequacy and a renewed sense of excitement. Here the group gains insight and understanding and learns how to give feedback. There is increased open and authentic interaction, with "playfulness" emerging as an "extension of sharing" (Ettin, Vaughan, & Fiedler, 1987). The earlier reliance on the leader shifts to a heavy reliance between members. There is also less of a struggle against the leader, other group members and the task. This shift in attitude increases productivity and helps to fan the lit fires of positive feelings.

In therapy or training groups, this is indeed an exciting time for the group, particularly if in most of the group's life the experience has been frustrating if not anxiety-provoking and unpleasant. This period in the life of the group is short. While work has been going on all the time, particularly if the focus is to learn about groups or learn about self, actual productive work accompanied by positive feelings of high hopes, embodies a relatively short span of time. A pitfall often experienced in the work stage is that of a preoccupation with the social-emotional interests of the group. The danger lies in putting more energy into the building of the relationships than the task at hand. As the group begins to get side-tracked and as the social takes over the task, it begins to enter a less productive stage. Aimlessness may descend upon the group with the earlier excitement shifting to anxiety and a sense of restlessness.

While enthusiasm and morale are restored in the group during this production stage, it does not mean that the group does not return or "re-experience unrealistic hopes or recurring frustration." When this happens, however, the group is able to recognize this more quickly and shift out of it more easily. Morale in the group can drop if members have extended themselves too much or if they have been involved in rather boring and mundane work. Furthermore, it can happen at the loss of a member due to unforeseen circumstances or when the task has no end in sight. When this takes place, the group begins to become less productive and the earlier dissatisfaction experienced in the previous stage gets revisited.

Roles surfacing during this stage are both task and maintenance. In the task realm, we see frequent use of defining the problem, testing feasibility and a free exchange of giving and seeking opinions and information. In the maintenance realm, additional roles of mediating-harmonizing and orienting-facilitating begin to emerge. These roles are particularly key as this stage is "normally marked by member-to-member discussion and confrontation" (Ettin, Vaughan, & Fiedler, 1987). Individual roles (non-functional) while in evidence, only surface when the group begins to get bogged down or when members' needs have been ignored.

Throughout this stage, the group continues to experience periods of mild fluctuations of feelings of "pleasantness to unpleasantness." In general, however, positive morale climbs during this period and then reaches a plateau with work level being medium to high.

Summary of Shifts in Morale, Work Level and Roles during the Production Stage

Group Development Stage	Morale	Work Level	Task Roles	Maintenance Roles	Individual Roles (Non-Functional
Production	High or positive morale As it rises it reaches a plateau	Medium to high Time is used efficiently and the group works more effectively	Defining the problem Giving and seeking information and testing feasibility	Coordinating Supporting-encouraging Following Mediating-harmonizing	Rarely any in evidence

FIGURE III-5

TERMINATION

<table>
<tr>
<td>

Key Features

</td>
<td>

- **Assessment and realistic appraisal of task**
- **Morale fluctuates depending on task completion**
- **Personal nature of task makes termination difficult**
- **Period of mourning, sadness and reminiscing**

</td>
</tr>
</table>

What is termination? Why is it so important? What does it represent? These are important questions. For while termination signals the ending process for the group, it does not necessarily signify that it comes at the end of its development (Anderson, 1985). This distinction, while seemingly trivial, is anything but!

The "ending process for the group" means that it has reached its end because it has completed its task or because the allotted time has run out, whereas, "end of the group's development" signifies that the group has completed its life cycle, having gone through the various stages mentioned previously. Thus, if termination comes **after** task completion or **after** the group has been able to work through aspects of interdependence and cohesion, members will benefit enormously from this stage. If however, the group terminates **before** this stage has been reached, and while in the midst of the dissatisfaction stage or while still in the midst of the production stage, the outcomes are quite negative. For example, members may start coming in later and later, or don't come at all. The disintegration that follows adversely influences members' future orientation in other new group situations.

As in most of the stages, the process in the termination stage varies according to the focus of the group. In task, work groups, committees, and learning groups, this stage can be quite short, ranging from part of a session to just a few minutes, particularly if relationships are habitual. Feelings generated here, have less to do with loss and closure and more to do with pride or disappointment, depending on whether or not the task mandated to the group has been successfully achieved.

In short term problem-solving groups, while the process is similar to that of the above, there is one exception. If the nature of the task the group has been working on is personal, the experience of loss and sadness is stronger. There may be some reluctance to bring closure with members talking of reconnecting to do further work at a later date.

In therapy or training groups, this process is quite complex since termination forms part of the task with which the group needs to grapple. Since the nature of the work has been personal and since the group has been privy to some painful, critical and demanding encounters amongst members, bonding at a very deep level has taken place. This makes closure particularly difficult. The risk-taking that has taken place and the vulnerability that has been displayed as disclosure at a deep level has been experienced, further add to difficulty with closure. In some groups, the stress surrounding termination may lead to a return to the dependence of the orientation stage or to the anger of the dissatisfaction stage. In general, however, this period is one of mourning, sadness and reminiscing.

In all these groups, termination involves coming to terms with both its accomplishments and limitations in relation to the task. This means a period of assessment and realistic appraisal of what has been gained and what yet needs to be done. Where the experience has been positive and the task satisfactorily completed, members experience increased self-esteem, whereas failure to complete the task satisfactorily leads to decreased self-esteem.

While work level may increase to cover up loss or to complete the task, generally it drops during this stage. Morale may dip or uplift, depending on whether the task has been completed, the way termination has been handled, and the success with which the group has moved through different stages. Roles appearing during this stage vary greatly. If the group is rushing to meet a deadline, maintenance roles drop with task becoming quite predominant. The reverse takes place, if the group has experienced some measure of success and satisfaction with the task. That is, task roles drop and maintenance rise. Individual roles may start to rise, especially those of digressing and blocking as members cover up feelings of loss, sadness and pride.

Summary of Shifts in Morale, Work Level and Roles during the Termination Stage

Group Development Stage	Morale	Work Level	Task Roles	Maintenance Roles	Individual Roles (Non-Functional)
Termination	High or low morale depending on the situation	Medium to low Period of assessment and realistic appraisal of task completion	Defining the problem Giving and seeking information and opinions If group is rushing to meet a deadline, there is high focus on the above roles When task is completed there is a low focus	Supporting-encouraging Following Mediating-harmonizing Orienting-facilitating If group is rushing to meet a deadline, there is a low focus on the above roles When task is completed, there is a high focus	Blocking Digressing

FIGURE III-6

Versatility of Group Development Stage Theory
How Lacoursiere's Group Development Stage Theory
Adapts Itself to Various Group Forms

a) Training for T-Groups

Focus:	To examine how groups function and participants behave
Membership:	Closed, 10-15 participants
Length of Group Life:	10-50 meetings, 1-2 hours in length
Group Leader:	Trainer, Consultant, Facilitator

General Developmental Characteristics

In training or T-Groups, group developmental stages are more clearly delineated due to decreased defensiveness and fostering of increased expression of hopes, fears, feelings, etc.

Orientation	Task and socio-emotional areas of behaviour are hard to separate. Orientation may take longer since task is difficult to define and achieve. Thus, aspects of orientation may be discernible half-way through the group experience. If participation is forced, there is negative orientation.
Dissatisfaction	Group more commonly gets arrested at this stage. Here anger is directed toward both leader and group members.
Resolution	Cohesion and the development of group oriented norms encourage decrease in animosity towards leader, and increase in cooperation amongst members towards goal achievement.
Production	Since task is hard to define and skills more difficult to acquire, a distinct production stage with a high level of work and positive feelings about it, may be a relatively small part of group life.
Termination	Termination becomes part of the task with feelings of loss examined as part of the process. Generally this is a difficult task.

FIGURE III-7

71

Versatility of Group Development Stage Theory
How Lacoursiere's Group Development Stage Theory
Adapts Itself to Various Group Forms

b) Therapy Groups

Focus: Personal exploration and understanding of one's motivation, behaviour and action

Membership: Open-ended, Usually 5-8 patients

Length of Group Life: Indeterminate, Usually long term, e.g., 1-2 years, 1-2 hours weekly, or more frequent

Group Leader: Therapist, Psychiatrist

General Developmental Characteristics

In therapy groups, developmental stages are more clearly delineated due to decreased defensiveness and fostering of increased expression of hopes, fears, feelings, etc.

Orientation	Task and socio-emotional areas of behaviour are hard to separate. Task is more difficult to define, thus, orientation lasts a longer percentage of time and blends into subsequent stages. This stage can be even more prolonged because of the open-ended nature of group. Sometimes it starts with a honeymoon period which is short lived. If participation is involuntary, there is negative orientation with person or group, never reaching the production stage.
Dissatisfaction	Group more commonly gets arrested at this stage. Here, anger is directed toward both leader and group members.
Resolution	Cohesion and the development of group oriented norms, encourage decrease animosity towards leader and increase, cooperation amongst members towards goal achievement.
Production	Since task is hard to define and skills more difficult to acquire, a distinct production stage with a high level of wand positive feelings about it, maybe a relatively small part of group life. In excessively long term groups, production fluctuates because of changes in members' goals or changes in membership.
Termination	Termination becomes part of the task, with feelings of loss examined as part of the process. Since these groups are quite long, there is probably a longer termination stage.

FIGURE III-8

Versatility of Group Development Stage Theory
How Lacoursiere's Group Development Stage Theory
Adapts Itself to Various Group Forms

c) Short Term Problem-Solving Groups

Focus: Group addresses a wide range of problems usually without a clear-cut solution

Membership: Closed, Ideally 3-6 persons, Maximum 20 persons

Length of Group Life: 1-10 meetings, Regular meetings with varying lengths

Group Leader: Usually no formal leader

General Developmental Characteristics

Orientation	Task and socio-emotional areas of behaviour are quite distinct. Orientation may be quick, particularly if task is impersonal, concrete and clear-cut.
Dissatisfaction	Is usually mild. If task is too vague or unrealistic, group can get stuck in this stage with anger directed at authority figures.
Resolution	May not be a distinct stage, since time pressure exerts an influence on what needs to be accomplished.
Production	Usually most of the time is spent in this stage.
Termination	May not be an issue, but strongly influenced by task completion. Termination tends to be short - less than a meeting, or maybe just a few minutes.

FIGURE III-9

Versatility of Group Development Stage Theory
How Lacoursiere's Group Development Stage Theory
Adapts Itself to Various Group Forms

d) Task / Work Groups & Committees

Focus: Group works on a given task with a specific mandate

Membership: Closed, Approximately 3-10 persons

Length of Group Life: Short term, Approximately 1-10 meetings, Regular meetings
                              with varying hours

Group Leader: Usually no assigned leader, May have a chairperson

General Developmental Characteristics

Orientation	Task and socio-emotional areas of behaviour are quite distinct. Orientation may be short, particularly if task is clear and mandate specific.
Dissatisfaction	If task is too vague and unrealistic, group may not move beyond this stage, with anger directed at authority figures. Sometimes the initial stage of high enthusiasm gives way to frustration and disgruntlement when recommendations are not heeded. Unrest and rivalry may appear.
Resolution	Expectations get adjusted to fit the realities of the task and the restrictions of the situation. If task is clear and realistic, this stage is often skipped and passed over.
Production	When task is easy to define, and realistic to carry out, group spends most of the time in this stage.
Termination	This is influenced by task completion and how long the group has been in existence. Termination may not be an issue, if relationships are habitual. This stage may only last a few hours.

FIGURE III-10

74

Versatility of Group Development Stage Theory
How Lacoursiere's Group Development Stage Theory
Adapts Itself to Various Group Forms

e) Learning Groups

Focus: Group brought together with the shared goal of
                           fostering learning around a specific goal

Membership: Usually closed, 3-6 persons

Length of Group Life: Short term, Approximately 1-10 meetings, Weekly
                           meetings with varying hours

Group Leader: No assigned leader

General Developmental Characteristics

Orientation	Task and socio-emotional areas of behaviour are quite distinct. Initial high enthusiasm. Orientation may be short, particularly if task is clear and skills achievable. If participation is compulsory, there is negative orientation.
Dissatisfaction	If task is too vague or unrealistic, group can get stuck with anger directed at authority figures. When members vary widely in their ability to contribute, conflict and unrest appear.
Resolution	Cohesion, acceptance of differences, and pooling of resources begin to appear.
Production	Group spends most of the time in this stage. Production is difficult to assess as the processing of learning extends past the group's life.
Termination	This is influenced by task completion and how long the group has been in existence. Termination may not be an issue, if relationships are habitual. If nature of learning is personal, termination may be more difficult.

FIGURE III-11

75

KEY FEATURES OF LACOURSIERE'S THEORY

1. **Negative orientation**

2. **Disequilibrium**

3. **Morale**

4. **Getting stuck in the dissatisfaction stage**

5. **Variations to the life cycle model**

6. **Individual life cycles and the group**

1. Negative Orientation

Lacoursiere emphasizes this point, as it not only influences a participant's entry into a group, but also her/his willingness to produce and become a resourceful and effective member. However, while this invariably influences willingness to take on responsibility, it does not influence ability.

Negative orientation is experienced when participants are coerced, pressured, forced or required to attend a particular group, class, committee, task force, etc. The mandatory nature of the attendance negatively influences orientation, which in turn negatively influences motivation and participation. Thus, this stage begins with testing and resistance, and in some cases (e.g., court orders), acting out and rebellion.

An example of frequently experienced negative orientation is seen in university where students are required to register for certain courses in order to fulfill academic requirements for their degree. Orientation in such situations is usually negative with the student far from experiencing positive expectations, reluctantly registers for the required course. This becomes even more difficult when the required attendance is that of a course involving one's personal engagement, or the data studied in the course constitutes one's personal experience (Levine, 1971). Anger and hostility are close at hand, and the resistance experienced interferes with the student's learning process.

76

Sometimes negative orientation gets blended into severe dissatisfaction, influencing healthy movement in the resolution, production, and termination stages. When this negative orientation stage blends into the dissatisfaction stage, the whole first part of the group's life is experienced in a negative way. Work level is minimal to poor, with the group experiencing low positive morale. For a group that is experiencing this process, entry into the production stage must be preceded by a clearly observable resolution stage. With some participants or groups who become arrested in the dissatisfaction stage i.e., never reaching the resolution stage, demoralization sets in. This creates the basis for future negative orientation in other groups, with statements such as "I don't expect to get much out of this group experience."

Thus, the resolution stage is faced with the daunting task of not only resolving the usual dissatisfaction with the task, and the concomitant unrealistic expectation of members, but also the resistance about their being in the group in the first place.

Most groups have a blend of participants along this continuum with a concentration toward one of the extremes. Depending on which extreme this concentration falls on, the orientation stage of the group may be positive or negative.

Continuum Illustrating Entry Points
Influencing the Orientation Stage

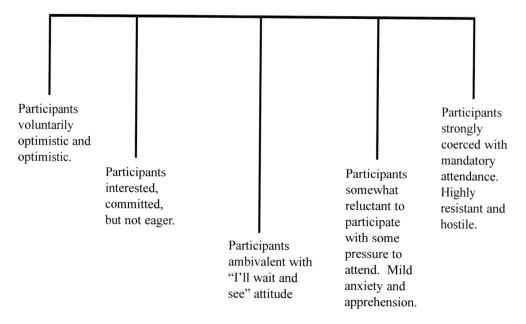

FIGURE III-12

2.   Disequilibrium

The concept of disequilibrium is pivotal to Lacoursiere's Life Cycle of Groups. It not only shapes the dissatisfaction stage, but is the basis for understanding its passage through difficult stages. As we have seen, central to disequilibrium is encountering experiences and concepts that are incongruent with one's expectations and preconceptions (Kass, 1983). As these get shaken, disconfirmation is experienced, often creating further disorientation, bewilderment and vulnerability. The culture shock that follows is difficult to handle and for a while members either try to quell and screen themselves off from realities that disconfirm, or they try to respond to the challenge for change, whilst at the same time attempting to hold on to their initial expectations.

It is this struggle of forces pulling in opposite directions and the accompanying feelings generated from this "rude awakening" that characterizes much of the process in the dissatisfaction stage. And while the "bursting of the bubble" is located in one stage (dissatisfaction), the process leading up to it (orientation), and the process leading out of it (resolution, production, termination) are all interconnected. This concept suggests that, the growth of a group begins with the experience of a dilemma or disconfirming information, and that the early encounters experienced in the dissatisfaction stage, if worked through, serve to start an unfolding process of learning and heightened awareness that can potentially lead to productive work through the life cycle of the group.

3.   Morale

Lacoursiere presents his group developmental life cycle model in terms of a "morale curve" to summarize shifts in the socio-emotional tone as the group moves through different stages. According to him, morale is a healthy mental stage or positive attitude that permits the **individual** in the face of adversity to maintain optimism and purposeful action. When this is applied to the **individual in the group**, it is very powerful for it means that the individual brings to the group an attitude of resolve, and a mental state that shows grit and mettle in the face of difficulties. Here, individuals are likely to wholeheartedly embrace the group, displaying confidence in it and in their own role as members. When the dynamic is further applied to the group as a whole, the **morale** is seen as a healthy mental state existing in relation to the task and the work that needs to be accomplished. Shifts in morale suggest that over a span of time, morale can lower, shatter, climb, strengthen, sink, or wane. Usually significant turning points in a group bring about these shifts in morale.

What are some of these turning points? For example, we note that groups usually start orientation with a positive, if not high morale, and that it is only when they are confronted with the realities of the task, that dissatisfaction sets in and a lowering of morale takes place. This turning point acts as a filter influencing hitherto what was a high morale. As the group struggles and tries to resolve its difficulties, and addresses the incongruities it is facing, morale begins to climb,

78

signaling that the group has entered the resolution stage. However, it is only when the group begins to address and own its issues that morale begins to climb. Once the group has settled down to work, morale continues to slowly rise, but soon reaches a plateau. Unless the group is confronted with further obstacles, the plateau continues.

As the group enters the termination stage, we note either a rise or fall in morale. If it has been able to complete the task successfully, there is a rise in morale. If the task remains incomplete or inadequately executed, there is a fall in morale. In groups where the task is related to personal growth and personal data, task completion may not be accompanied by a rise in morale. In fact, there may be a drop in morale. The reason for this, is that looming ahead is closure and the disbanding of the group. The dip or uplift in morale has much to do with how this termination stage is managed. If members are able to go beyond their sadness of closure and permit themselves to experience pride in their work, then morale rises. If, however, the group gets caught up in its loss rather than in its pleasure of a job well done, morale dips.

Situational morale is not uncommon with some groups experiencing high morale while, working on one task, but low morale whilst working on another. Generally, however, as long as the group has clear and realistic goals, high morale is to be expected. High morale can also exist in the group even though some individuals are experiencing low morale and vice versa. What is more common however, is the degree to which a person's morale can depend on the morale of others in a group.

Pseudo morale - This is more commonly experienced in therapy and training groups, where members put on a "face to meet the other faces." And by this, I mean, members cover up their real feelings of anger, frustration, disappointment, etc., and pretend that "all is just fine," giving little indication of their true feelings. This is most often seen when the person in question finds it difficult to make a statement, suggesting the opposite of what has been stated by the group. Hence a person who seems enthusiastic about the experience may in fact inwardly be downgrading it.

Shifts in Morale Occuring in Different Stages

	Orientation	Dissatisfaction	Resolution	Production	Termination
Morale	High or positive morale	Low morale

Here morale falls well below the neutral baseline. | Morale begins to climb | High or positive morale

Here morale remains at a plateau. | High or low morale |
| **Observations** | Members enter the group with enthusiasm, hope, and high expectations.

Negative or low morale expected if group begins with negative orientation. | Here morale hits its lowest point.

Negative forces outweigh positive ones as members encounter experiences that are incongruent with their reality. | As the group begins to sort through issues of expectations and task realities, morale rises.

If resolution does not take place, morale remains low and demoralization sets in. | Here morale continues to rise but is never as high as during orientation stage.

Demoralization can occur when the task is too difficult, is boring, or been done for too long. | Here morale may drop or uplift, depending upon the personal significance of the experience, the task success, or the ability of the group to deal with closure. |

FIGURE III-13

Low morale occurs primarily in the stages of negative orientation, dissatisfaction and termination.

4.   Getting Stuck in the Dissatisfaction Stage

While getting stuck is possible in any stage, it is more likely to occur during the dissatisfaction stage, i.e., the unpleasant stage. The list below is derived from my experiences as an academic involved in student and peer groups, and as a consultant involved in training groups in the professional world.

1.   When members in the group are unable and unwilling to put aside their differences and focus on the task.

2.   When the group refuses to become more realistic about the task at hand, or change to more realistic goals.

3.   When the task assigned to the group is vague and impossible to define.

4.   When members vary widely in their ability to contribute.

5.   When the task assigned to the group is unrealistic and impossible to fulfil within the time frame allotted.

6.   When the task assigned to the group is unrealistic because the skills are not adequate to the task to be fulfilled.

7.   When a group refuses to acknowledge and own the process they are experiencing, i.e., avoiding to address the inconsistencies that confront them, and attempt to deny the experienced confusion and vulnerability.

8.   When the needs in the group are incompatible with the task needed to be accomplished.

9.   When members consistently let down the group by not taking on necessary responsibilities, or by not fulfilling responsibilities they have promised to take on.

5.   Variations to the Life Cycle Model

Lacoursiere's model of group development delineates five stages of group growth: orientation, dissatisfaction, resolution, production and termination. Depending on the focus, the significance of the experience, and the duration of the group, the resolution and termination stages are sometimes less clearly visible or even omitted. These two stages become unobtrusive for different reasons.

In the resolution stage, we note the following: when the dissatisfaction stage has been less pronounced, short and fairly smooth, the necessity for a distinct or separate resolution stage is not there. Thus, the ending of the dissatisfaction stage blends uninterrupted into production, with work on the task beginning to take place almost immediately. This process is most often seen in task and work groups, committees and short term problem-solving groups, where time is of essence and where the focus is less personal.

In the termination stage, we note the following: When the group has met for only a short while or is working under a deadline, when its focus is impersonal, and when the relationships are habitual, termination is barely visible. Given the preceding conditions, this stage sometimes takes only a few minutes for wrap-up during the last session. This process is most commonly observed in task and work groups, committees, and short term problem-solving groups. In these groups termination often does not even feature as a stage, with the group ending abruptly once the task is completed.

6.   Individual Life Cycles and the Group

So far, we have examined different stages which the group experiences as it goes through its life cycle. What we have not examined is how an individual's cycle can differ from that of the group's life cycle. Lacoursiere suggests that individuals construct their own life cycle in a group, and while these individual cycles influence the group, it is only when "several" members simultaneously go through the same cycle that the group is said to be in a particular stage. Whether "several" means 25%, 50%, or even 75% of the group is not clear.

Individual cycles - Most people at some point in their lives have experienced the feeling of being outside of the group's rhythm or "out of sync" with the rest of the group. For example, some people may experience the orientation stage as boring, useless and unproductive, whereas others may experience it as exciting, helpful and important. For some, the dissatisfaction stage is quickly dismissed as "trivial nonsense," or "much ado about nothing," whereas others may experience it as a "death blow" from which it is difficult to recover. For still others, the resolution stage may be tedious and a waste of time, whereas for others, it may be a highlight and a turning point. For some people, the production stage is a time where they are able to sustain and maintain a high level of task focus, whereas others drift off and give up. Some handle the termination stage with ease; others experience it as stressful and something to be avoided.

Why those differences? What determines these individual life cycles? To start with, we know that unfinished business from one experience interferes and influences the next experience. For example, poorly handled terminations, negatively influence other orientations. Similarly, anticipation of the next orientation may influence the current termination stage. We also know that people, who have been in groups that have been arrested during the dissatisfaction stage, usually enter new group situations with low expectations, discomfort and reluctance. They are also unlikely to experience the dissatisfaction stage with the same negative intensity as others who have come into the experience with high expectations, hopes and enthusiasm. Similarly, people who have experienced the success of overcoming obstacles in one group situation are more likely to face new obstacles in another group with a positive attitude, whereas others with a previous negative experience are more likely to give up, hold back or be pessimistic about it.

In addition to the above, we also know that a person's developmental stage and life cycle issues interact with, and influence their participation in a group. For example people who are experiencing termination difficulties in their personal life, may find the termination of a group in which strong ties have been developed, hard to cope with; they may do their best to avoid it, make light of it, or become demoralized. Or, a person who is experiencing severe dissatisfaction on the job may well find it difficult to participate with eagerness and enthusiasm in a work related task group. Thus, investment and commitment may be lower than someone who has just been promoted, publicly honoured or listened to with respect.

As we can see, the different individual cycles within a group are limitless and the reason for their existence is countless. What we do know, is that they add to the complexity of a group, influencing, interfering, and interacting with the developmental life cycle of a group.

STRENGTHS AND WEAKNESSES

One major limitation of Lacoursiere's model is the lack of clear data about open-ended and short-term groups. Considering the frequency with which practitioners give leadership to both these types of groups (e.g., hospital, social service agencies, etc.) some analysis addressing issues related to the developmental life cycle of these groups, would have been useful. While Lacoursiere makes mention of open-ended groups and the length of life cycles as conditions that affect group developmental stages, he does not go further into this.

Despite the above weakness, Lacoursiere's framework is an extremely valuable life cycle model of group development. It is practical, flexible and instrumental. His discussion on negative orientation and its ripple effect provides a significant contribution in the area of non-voluntary attendance in groups. In addition, his observation of arrestation in the development of a group is extremely helpful, since most group development theories do not even make a reference to its possibility, focusing only on the development of the group (Kuypers, Davies, Glaser, 1986). His discussion on arrestation is constructive in that it draws attention to the possibilities of a group not achieving a complete developmental sequence. It also lends clarity into why many individuals find it difficult to enter new group situations. Further to the above, Lacoursiere's presentation of morale as a dynamic changing characteristic is a useful concept for those who seek intervention guidelines from this model. Lastly, his wide data base e.g., inclusion of more "natural" work groups from which he has drawn to support the ideas for his framework, gives breadth and potency to his model, for it can be applied in both the workplace and in social, therapeutic, and educational settings.

PERSONAL NOTES ON LACOURSIERE

REFERENCES

Anderson, J. (1985). Working with groups: Little known facts that challenge well known myths. *Small Group Behaviour*, 16 (3), 267-283.

Dies, R. (1984). The life cycle of groups: Group developmental stage theory. *International Journal of Group Psychotherapy*, 34 (2), 300-302.

Ettin, M. F., Heiman, M. L., & Kopel, S. A. (1988). Group building: Developing protocols for psycho-educational. *Groups, 12* (4), 205-225.

Ettin, M.F., Vaughan, E., & Fiedler, N. (1987). Managing group process in nonprocess groups: Working with the theme-centred psychoeducational group. *Groups, 11,* (3), 177-193.

Gruner, L. R. (1984). Membership composition of open and closed therapeutic groups. *Small Group Behaviour, 16* (2), 222-232.

Hill, W. F., & Gruner, L. (1973). A study of development in open and closed groups. *Small Group Behaviour, 4,* 355-381.

Karterud, S., & Foss, T. (1989). The group emotionality rating system: A modification of Thelen's method of assessing emotionality in groups. *Small Group Behaviour, 20* (2), 131-150.

Kass, R. (1983). *The apology stance in the learning process.* Unpublished doctoral dissertation, University of Toronto.

Kuypers, B. C., Davies, D., & Glaser, K. H. (1986). Developmental arrestation in self-analytic groups. *Small Group Behaviour, 17 (3)*, 269-302.

Lacoursiere, R. (1974). A group method to facilitate learning during the stages of a psychiatric affiliation. *International Journal of Group Psychotherapy, 24,* 342-351.

Lacoursiere, R. (1980). *The life cycle of groups: Group developmental stage theory.* New York: Human Sciences Press.

Lacoursiere, R. (1982). A group method in clinical legal education. *Canadian Journal of Psychiatry, 27 (3)*, 253-254.

Schopler, J. H., & Galinsky, M. J. (1982). *The life cycle of groups: Group developmental stage theory. Social Service Review, 56,* 674-675.

Schopler, J. H., & Galinsky, M. J. (1990). Can open-ended groups move beyond beginnings? *Small Group Research, 21 (4),* 435-449.

IV. SCHUTZ'S THREE DIMENSIONAL THEORY OF INTERPERSONAL AND GROUP BEHAVIOUR

OVERVIEW

This theory of group development is derived from Schutz's interpersonal relations schema (Schutz, 1958, 1966, 1982) called the "Fundamental Interpersonal Relations Orientation" known as FIRO (rhymes with Cairo). This framework assumes that groups like individuals have three basic interpersonal needs, namely: inclusion, control and openness [1] and that these needs cover most of our interpersonal behaviour. Schutz further suggests that these basic needs influence group behaviour in that "they determine how we treat other people and how we want others to treat us" (Forsyth, 1999). Within a group context, Schutz suggests that a group moves from an initial concern with inclusion needs to focus on control issues and finally to openness. Groups pass through observable, cyclical phases of these needs. He also suggests that as a group nears termination it reverses the order with which it deals with its interpersonal needs, and retraces its passage from openness to control to inclusion (O-C-I).

Inclusion:

Refers to individuals' need to share, include and involve others in their activities. It also refers to their need to be recognized, connected, feel included, and be accepted by others.

Control:

Refers to individuals' need to influence, dominate, take charge, be responsible and have authority over others. It also refers to their need to be dependent, follow, have an anchor, be guided, and have others take over.

Openness:

Refers to individuals' need to trust, love, give emotional support and be authentic. It also refers to their need to feel safe, loveable, receive emotional support, and experience friendship.

---

[1] "**Affection**" to "**Openness**" - Originally, Schutz (1958, 1966) used *Affection* instead of *Openness* which he currently uses in his description of areas of interpersonal needs. After many years of using the FIRO instrument it became clear to him that *Affection* was not parallel to Inclusion and Control. In his revision of the original theory, Schutz has this to say about his theoretical revision and development, "*Affection* as a concept, is more related to feeling than to behaviour. Accordingly *Affection* now is identified by its essential behavioural ingredient, *Openness*" (Schutz, 1982).

Schutz's theory explains the interpersonal underworld of small groups and how they offer members a way to satisfy these basic needs. His instrument FIRO-B (B=behaviour) measures how individuals relate to other group members in terms of what they choose to express towards them ("**Expressed**" behaviour) and what they wish to receive from them ("**Wanted**" behaviour). The difference is in the direction of the behaviour or feeling, e.g., "**toward others**" or "**toward self**."

Schutz also argues that people's interpersonal behaviour will be similar to the behaviours they experienced in their earliest relationships. Dimock (1967), in his article on "Individual Growth," eloquently builds on Schutz's premise. He stresses the importance of a child's first year in terms of "**inclusion**" and belonging. He describes how, between the ages of four and six months, "a hungry baby will grow quiet and show signs of pleasure when he hears someone coming, in anticipation of being cuddled and fed." Dimock describes the infant's next developmental stage as a time when a child tries to learn how he is able to influence and "**control**" some of the things that happen to him. He describes the typical behaviour of the "terrible two" who, "….through many types of negative behaviour such as temper tantrums, resistance to toilet training, and frequent use of the word 'no,' experiments with his control dimension to see how much influence he can have over his parents and his environment." Dimock continues to trace the development of these three interpersonal needs into the adolescent teenage years, into the experience of peer pressure, the desire for membership in a peer group, the development of intimacy ("**openness**"), and the search for personal identity. He concludes his article by stating that further development of "these areas continue throughout life."

Since a group is made up of individuals the argument follows that groups like individuals have the same basic interpersonal needs. In a broad sense they become "arenas in which individual needs are satisfied or frustrated" (Beebe & Masterson, 2000). Over the years I have found this developmental framework tremendously useful both in my teaching activities at the University and my training activities in the field. It has provided a useful framework in the design of courses and workshops, in the planning of team meetings and in my work with colleagues in the field.

The initial part of this chapter is a summary description of Schutz's theory of interpersonal and group behaviour and the latter part calls attention to various basic issues related to aspects of this framework. The following description assumes an on-going group of 6-20 persons with a particular focus, relatively little personal information about fellow members, and differing perceptions of the task at hand and of the methods to be used for reaching the identified task. This description also assumes that the group is starting out and that the development of the group is greatly influenced by its composition, particularly if certain skills and resources are limited.

The reader is encouraged to bear in mind that while the events described below are representative of what may occur as a group develops, each group is unique and must be "understood in terms of exceptions and in terms of when, how and why changes in development occur" (Napier & Gershenfeld, 1999).

Manifestations of Inclusion, Control, and Openness:
Individual Characteristics and Development Needs

Basic Characteristic	Basic Feelings	Central Concern	Central Issue	Optimal Balance	Physical Compass
Inclusion	How I feel about my significance	Achieving just the right amount of contact between self and others	In - Out	**Presence:** Optimal inclusion of self	Going towards Drawing back
Control	How I feel about my competence	Achieving just the right amount of control over self and others	Top - Bottom	**Spontaneity:** Optimal control over self	Rising above Falling below
Openness	How I feel about my likeability	Achieving just the right amount of openness between self and others	Open -Closed	**Awareness:** Optimal openness to self	Reaching out Closing off

FIGURE IV-1

91

Summary of Central Expressions of
Inclusion, Control and Openness

Context	Inclusion	Control	Openness
1. **Phase**	Early	Middle	Mature
2. **Issue**	In or out	Top or Bottom	Near or far
3. **Interaction**	Encounter	Confront	Embrace
4. **Self-concept**	Significance	Competence	Lovability
5. **Preoccupation**	Prominence	Dominance	Closeness
6. **Fear**	Being ignored	Being humiliated	Being rejected
7. **Motivation**	Self-inclusion	Self-determination	Self-awareness
8. **Rigid Behaviour**	Loner/ Attention seeker	Never risks/ Over commits	Never gets close/ Immediately tries to get close
9. **Self-talk**	"Will anyone be interested in me?"	"Can I handle the responsibility?"	"Can I be 'me' in this group?"
10. **Focus**	Membership	Leadership	Fellowship
11. **Energy Level**	Anticipatory	Draining	Creative
12. **Emotional Climate**	Artificial	Charged	Permissive
13. **Predominant Theme**	Grope	Gripe	Group
14. **Communication**	Camouflaged	Distorted	Clear
15. **Productivity**	Low	Medium	High

FIGURE IV-2

```
┌─────────────────────────────────────┐
│                                      │
│            INCLUSION                 │
│                                      │
│      Achieving just the right amount of │
│        contact between self and others. │
│                                      │
│             "In - Out"               │
│                                      │
└─────────────────────────────────────┘
```

As the group starts, people bring with them a "mixed bag" of hopes, fears and expectations. It is through this lens that new members begin to listen, observe and take action. Uppermost in people's minds during this entry period is the desire to connect, the wish to belong and the need to be accepted by the group. The central concern is the acceptance of the individual by the group and the perception as to whether one is "in" or "out" of the group. What is essential here is not whether the member is **just in or out**, the issue is if the member has achieved the place s/he wants to be and whether the group accommodates and/or respects that wish. What is important to note, is that it is the inclusion issues, and not the task issues that "get the ball rolling." Thus the preoccupation at this phase is one of "prominence and not dominance" (Schutz, 1982).

As introductions take place and the work of the group begins members vary in their interpersonal ways of achieving the desired amount of contact between self and others. The question at play is "how much do I let all of me participate in what I am doing?" Fear more than trust prevails; in an effort to reduce tensions and anxieties members display a wide range of participation behaviours as they try to deal with these boundary issues.

As limits concerning the amount of contact and interaction get established, extreme and rigid interpersonal behaviours begin to appear. Some members display under-social and over-social behaviours. For example (Schutz, 1966, Waterman & Rogers, 1996, Wilson, 1996) the interpersonal behaviour of the **"under-social"** individuals is one of being withdrawn, watchful and guarded, directing their energies toward self-preservation with their preference for privacy often being misinterpreted as lack of interest in others or even arrogance. On the other hand the inter-personal behaviour of the **"over-social"** individuals is one of being talkative, glib and unrestrained with their eagerness to contribute often being misinterpreted as a wish to dominate. Dimock (1987) suggests that this **over** and **under** participation often becomes an issue in the group. In general this beginning period is one of heightened tension and caution coupled with hope and trepidation.

For most members, this inclusion process of group formation is a time for data gathering and information seeking about self and others. Here, group members are sorting out what is expected of them and what they expect of the group. This involves clarifying goals, assessing the qualifications of the designated leader, and determining the level and value of the content. All this helps members determine the nature and extent of their commitment and investment in the group. In short, many of the behaviours displayed in this early phase are individual rather than group oriented.

Characteristic of groups in this phase is the appearance of "goblet issues" (Schutz, 1966, p.170), a term borrowed from an analogy to a "cocktail party where people sometimes pick up their cocktail glass, or goblet, and figuratively use it to peer through to size up the other people at the party." These goblet issues hold little meaning for group members and are often pointless in content but serve as a catalyst for getting to know others. During the early sessions of a group, goblet issues appear in the form of the inevitable discussions about "the weather," the almost predictable question that follows an introduction of "do you know so and so?"and the inescapable exchange between students of "why are you taking this course?" or "what do you think of so and so?"

Goblet issues can take on the appearance of openness. For example deep disclosure in a support group, describing one's dysfunctional family can be used as a way to achieve acceptance and membership in the group. Often a goblet issue is made of the first decision confronting a group such as the time the group should convene for a coffee break. Each group finds its own goblet issue or a series of them and when not permitted this outlet, groups find another way of getting the same information.

During this phase, the work level of the group is low, participation is unequally distributed and commitment and investment to the group is being determined. The end of this phase sees the group with agreed upon rules of procedures, resistance to taking on new members and awareness by members as to who are solidly in the group, who are half-way in and who are on the fringe.

Some Ways of Showing Inclusion

Inviting or including others, moving towards others, showing interest in people though not in any particular person, demonstrating concern for undergone, joining activities with others, initiating and/or participating in conversations and discussions with others, joining social groups, participating in informal social gatherings and participating in the life of the group and/or enjoying doing things with the group.

Terms That May Suggest Positive Inclusion

Belong	Interaction	Orientation	Membership	Communicate	Mingle
Associate	Join	Acceptance	Friendship	Interest	Invite
Recognize	Approach	Exchange	Investment	Companionship	Connect
Relate	Recognition	Presence	Fellowship	Commitment	Involve
Significance	Respect	Support	Near	Acknowledgement	In

FIGURE IV-3

Terms That May Suggest Negative Inclusion

Outside	Overlooked	Excluded	Ignored	Over-compensate	Isolate
Distance	Loner	Alone	Anxiety	Separation	Sidelines
Detached	Withdrawn	Abandoned	Watchful	Exhibitionism	Guarded
Exclusion	Avoid	Late	Absent	Over-contribute	Far
Interrupting	Scorn	Outcast	Upstart	Under-contribute	Fringe

FIGURE IV-4

Summary of Key Behaviours and Feelings
Experienced in the Inclusion Phase

Behaviours Expressed	Feelings Experienced
Overly talkative	Anticipation
Withdrawn	Distrust
Exhibitionism	Excitement
Watchful	Anxiety
Polite facade	Hope
Status-seeking	Overwhelmed
Accommodating	Trepidation
Testing	Doubt
Guarded	Hesitation
Joining	Confusion
Cautious	Nervous
Following	Discomfort
Maintenance	Neglect
Supporting	Fear
Inviting	Energy

FIGURE IV-5

Profile Types Showing Rigidity in
Dealing with Inclusion Needs

Undersocial Avoids satisfying "Inclusion" needs	Oversocial Constantly tries to satisfy "Inclusion" needs
• Maintains distance between self and others • Always late at meetings • Regularly leaves group before it ends • Lacks involvement in and commitment to the life of the group • Scorns the group because of its superficiality • Insists on not being included • Has many conflicting engagements • Precedes each group session with "I'm sorry, but I can't stay very long" • Tries to constantly appear self-sufficient • Withdraws from social and interactive activities that involve the group	• Always wants to be included and/or seeking companionship • Asks startling questions • Forces oneself on the group • Name dropping • Overly talkative • Narcissistic absorption in the needs and interests of self to the point of being quite unaware of others • Plans activities that always involve togetherness • Always seeking recognition, fame, acclaim, reputation and/or success • Constantly interrupting • Constantly being the comedian

FIGURE IV-6

```
┌─────────────────────────────────────┐
│              CONTROL                 │
│                                      │
│     Achieving just the right amount of│
│       control over self and others.  │
│                                      │
│           "Top - Bottom"             │
└─────────────────────────────────────┘
```

Once a group has resolved some of its initial inclusion needs it begins to shift its attention to issues of power, influence, competence and authority. Procedures around decision-making begin to be questioned, authority concerns begin to surface and group members start challenging the lack of responsibility given them or resisting the amount of responsibility directed to them. The central concern is one of competence e.g. "will I be able to handle the responsibility?", "will I be able to cope?" and "will I be able to do the job required?" The pre-occupation is with self-determination, the avoidance of humiliation, and the fear of "being found out."

Hostilities grow, minor points are quibbled over, facades are dropped, members take or seek different roles, competition develops; power struggles often get displaced "onto the chalk." Here we note that members take on more fixed positions, issues get polarized, stereotypes begin to get disconfirmed, alignments get drawn and factions develop. It is within this atmosphere that a "pecking order" (Dimock 1987) is established. The main concern here is dominance, i.e., distribution of power and not prominence as seen in the inclusion phase.

During this period of turmoil and upheaval, some members try to dominate the group, while others resist or withdraw and still others comply and submit. Discontent prevails, energies get drained, tension rises and the general feeling is one of "getting nowhere" with complaints being heard such as "what a waste of time" and murmurs of "I can't stand groups." The desire for control varies along a continuum from wanting authority and influence over others to wanting others to have this control and responsibility. Schutz (1966, p. 22) suggests that in an argument one can distinguish an "inclusion seeker" from a "control seeker" in the following way: ".... the one seeking inclusion or prominence wants very much to be one of the participants in the argument" whereas the one seeking control wants to win the argument or at the very least be "on the same side as the winner" of the argument.

As limits concerning the amount of control get established, extreme and rigid interpersonal behaviours in the area of dominance begin to appear. Some members begin to display what Schutz (1966) calls "abdicratic" or "autocratic" behaviours. For example the "abdicrat" tends toward submission and abdication of responsibility. They tend to direct their energies toward independence and freedom from responsibility, often giving the impression of criticizing a lot but undertaking very little. On the other-hand the "autocrat" is a person whose interpersonal behaviour tends toward dominating and controlling others. They tend to overvalue competence, viewing every mistake as a disaster. Delegating and letting go of responsibility is difficult often imposing structure when it may have been better to go with the flow (Waterman & Rogers, 1996, Wilson, 1996).

It is not uncommon during this tense and difficult period for group members to entertain thoughts of leaving the group or confide to someone that they might not return. However, as this is part of the resistance, this rarely happens. What does happen is an "emotional withdrawal" evincing an attitude of "I may be here in body, but not in spirit."

In order to move ahead the group has to feel it can influence its own destiny, which means at some level the group needs to become responsible for its own decision-making, particularly in activities and procedures which influence its future existence.

Once leadership hierarchy is established and the group comes to terms with its issues of influence, responsibility and competence, and once it has established decision-making procedures, a paradigm shift takes place within the group. More evenly distributed leadership functions begin to emerge and shared responsibility begins to take place. As the group begins to tap the resources of various members and as norms appropriate to goal completion begin to get set, the work level rises and cohesion within the group increases.

It is within this context that group members begin to relax and enjoy the group. Their sense of accomplishment is high and no task seems too great. Comments such as "this is the best group," reflects part of the euphoria experienced by the group members during the latter part of this phase; realization that there is more to accomplish moves the group to the next phase.

Some Ways of Showing Control

Giving orders, being in charge or taking charge of situations, making decisions for self and others, seeking out situations where one has responsibility, getting others to do things and showing concern over the dictates of conscience and moral directives. In a group context this means being active by providing direction and influencing people's actions and decisions.

Terms That May Suggest Positive Control

Influence	Productive	Authority	Capable	Responsible	Leader
Power	Competent	Spontaneity	Risk-taking	Self-determination	Timing
Direction	Flexible	Self assurance	Autonomy	Willingness	Negotiate
Share	Structure	Adapt	Consolidate	Confident	Clarity
Flexibility	Coordination	Cooperation	Realistic	Interdependent	Balance

FIGURE IV-7

Terms That May Suggest Negative Control

Exploit	Rigid	Grudging	Defensive	Scapegoat	Neglect
Force	Hostile	Snide remarks	Sabotage	Hidden agenda	Rivalry
Interfere	Excessive	Anarchy	Punishment	Rebellion	Gossip
Bottom	Ingratiate	Plot	Conformity	Disregard	Conceal
Jockeying	Turmoil	Power struggle	Counter-dependent	Sub-grouping	Demand

FIGURE IV-8

Summary of Key Behaviours and Feelings
Experienced in the Control Phase

Behaviours Expressed	Feelings Experienced
Resistance	Inadequacy
Compliance	Distrust
Submission	Helplessness
Competition	Powerlessness
Blocking	Frustration
Dominating	Fatigue
Conforming	Apathy
Delegating	Resentment
Challenging	Suspicion
Consulting	Incompetence
Testing feasibility	Stuck
Influencing	Humiliation
Bickering	Threatened
Complaining	Pressured
Avoiding	Unsettling

FIGURE IV-9

Profile Types Showing Rigidity in
Dealing with Control Needs

Abdicrat Tends toward submission and abdication of power and responsibility	Autocrat Tends toward domination and resistance of control from other
• Rarely takes responsibility for making final decisions • Hesitates to "go along" • Gravitates toward those who take charge • Avoids situations of helplessness • Seeks out situations where there is no responsibility • Tends to be a loyal follower • Hesitates to undertake obligations • Avoids being in leadership or power positions • Constantly sits back and lets others take over • "Covers her/his ass"	• Makes decision for everyone • Works hard to get to the top • Controls situation and people and tries to master others. • Rarely lets go of control • Resists control and input from others • Seeks out situations of power and control • Quickly establishes position of control • Takes on too much responsibility • Concern with submission, discipline, authority, dominance and conformity • Makes unreasonable demands of others

FIGURE IV-10

OPENNESS

Achieving just the right amount of
openness between self and others.

"Open - Closed"

This phase is often remembered with great warmth, affection and feelings. Group members enter this period ready to work, ready to deal with each other as individuals, and ready to become more deeply involved and honest with one another. It is here that openness issues take centre stage with group members able to achieve an optimal degree of interchange and where personal feelings and opinions are communicated in a direct and honest way. The central concern is likeability/lovability and the preoccupation is "can I be 'me' in this group?", "how much of my personal self can I invest in this group?", "can I be creative in this group?" and "can I give and receive genuineness from this group?" It is important to note that the flow of openness is from "me to the individual members" and not necessarily vice versa. This new level of trust and openness releases the group's creative functional resources and unique abilities paving the way for productive problem-solving.

The working assumption in this phase is that openness is a necessary condition for the functioning of an effective group. Schutz (1984) suggests that it is only through the development of self-awareness that optimal openness to oneself and others can be achieved and channelled into the work of the group.

During this period dyadic relationships begin to develop and honest expressions of feelings begin to take place. As a sense of togetherness prevails, extreme and rigid interpersonal behaviours begin to be displayed with some members appearing "under-personal" and others "over-personal" (Schutz, 1966). For example the interpersonal behaviour of the under-personals is one of being emotionally distant. The human element is often not considered when analyzing problems and seeking solutions. Others may describe them as hard to know, reserved, self-contained, reflective, cautious, and even distant or intimidating. The interpersonal behaviour of the over-personals on the other hand is one of having trouble making their real needs clear. They often overwhelm others as they regularly personalize situations and issues, frequently invading privacy and boundaries (Waterman & Rogers, 1996, Wilson, 1996).

As group members become more open to each other and with each other, "who" is influencing "whom" is not an issue, for there is a willingness to be influenced by others and a readiness to influence others. This commitment to shared responsibility during this period is such that being delegated a task is not a source of contention but a source of genuine appreciation. In fact it is during this phase that members increasingly volunteer to take on tasks. Thus, working towards meeting a group goal is seen as a corporate responsibility and not relegated to the group leader or to a few powerful members. As responsibilities begin to get shared and as leadership begins to shift between members, the role differentiation emphasized earlier between group leader and group members lessens in importance and a more natural and informal dialogue begins to emerge.

As the group starts paying less attention to the status hierarchy within its ranks and more attention to the ideas and abilities of its members, encouragement of individual differences begins to occur. This results in less pressure on those with divergent or conflicting views and more opportunities for creative minorities to emerge. With this more accepting environment, the need for majority vote gradually decreases as group members become aware of the relationship between support of a decision and a process that provides for full participation in reaching a decision. This awareness moves the group to a more active use of consensual validation despite its sometimes slow and belaboured process.

During this phase there is a genuine effort to look at concerns, discover resources and avoid personalizing issues that occurred earlier. As abilities and skills within the group begin to be creatively used and as group members become more actively conscious of their role in contributing to the success of the group, investment in the group rises and attraction for the group increases. As trust begins to build, opposing opinions are sought after as part of the clarification process. This ushers in a period in which members openly share feelings, state opinions, make suggestions and test the feasibility of proposed solutions. As the data available for problem-solving rapidly increases, task and maintenance roles become more balanced and the work and confidence level of the group rises.

As closure sets in, the group retraces its passage[2] and focuses on their initial encounter with each other. This leads to a period of reflection on the leadership and communication patterns that facilitated or inhibited the group. This "processing" often results in the reminiscing of what it had been like to initially join the group and delving into why certain issues had been resisted or why certain decisions had been blocked or readily accepted. The awareness that the group will soon disband and that group members are dispersing in different directions often propels members to finalize closure with exchange of addresses, phone numbers and e-mails signifying that certain contacts will be maintained in the future.

---

[2] For elaboration on this concept, see section on Key Features "Reversal and retracing of the cycle" (p. 110).

When a group is able to end its existence at this phase it has been able to reach maturity and cohesiveness and has been able to experience growth and learning in a healthy and powerful way.

Some Ways of Showing Openness

Sharing creative resources and unique abilities, accepting and expecting openness, initiating and receiving feedback, delighting in the experience and in the company of others, sharing anger and disappointment, disclosing deep feelings, showing affection, narrowing the gap between "what I express and what I want", showing flexibility and willingness to change and seeing conflict as a positive force and an opportunity to problem-solve.

Terms That May Suggest Positive Openness

Personal	Honesty	Direct	Real	Forthright	Laughter
Overt	Intensity	Embrace	Readily	Close	Pairing off
Secure	Potential	Mutuality	Sincerity	Lovable	Disconcertment
Creative	Energy	Innermost	Expressive	Transparent	Responsiveness
Warmth	Profound	Candor	Integrated	Near	Comfortable

FIGURE IV-11

Terms That May Suggest Negative Openness

Closed	Avoid	Covert	Distant	Safeguard	Impersonal
Distrust	Indirect	Devour	Superficial	Withhold	Casual
Devious	Secret	Possessive	Deprive	Intrude	Polarization
Disinterest	Far	Dispassionate	Smother	Overwhelm	Non-selective
Cover up	Insincere	Ambiguous	Side whispers	Double message	Inappropriate

FIGURE IV-12

Summary of Key Behaviours and Feelings
Experienced in the Openness Phase

Behaviours Expressed	Feelings Experienced
Feedback	Satisfaction
Dialogue	Warmth
Openness	Affection
Rapport	Trust
Collaboration	Anger
Active listening	Disillusionment
Sharing	Fulfilment
Perspective Taking	Enjoyment
Problem-solving	Enthusiasm
Authenticity	Good will
Affirmation	Potency
Transparency	Lovable
Clarity	Safe
Disclosure	Genuineness
Reciprocate	Intimacy

FIGURE IV-13

Profile Types Showing Rigidity in
Dealing with Openness Phase

Underpersonal Tends toward avoiding close, personal and open relations with others	Overpersonal Tends toward becoming overly close, personal and open with others
• Engages in superficial interaction • Avoids and distrusts closeness • Rarely shares concerns or observations • Chooses to remain silent in areas of personal awareness • Keeps thoughts and feelings to self • Rarely responds to questions of personal disclosure • Gives indication of not wanting to get emotionally involved • Always thinks twice before disclosing • Reluctant to engage in feedback • Neither seeks nor accepts close relations	• Quick to disclose personal information and observations • Immediately tries to get close to others • Constantly reveals and divulges feelings • Regularly personalizes situation and issues • Strives to create a personal and intimate atmosphere in all situations • Does not show respect for privacy • Smothers others with affection • Constantly confides in others • Frequently invades boundaries • Discloses inappropriate information

FIGURE IV-14

KEY FEATURES OF SCHUTZ'S THEORY

1. **Sequence is temporal**

2. **Phases are not distinct**

3. **Phases are not always reached or completed**

4. **Dimensions get revisited and recycled**

5. **Reversal and retracing of the cycle**

6. **Individual versus group**

7. **Importance of the inclusion phase**

8. **The "pain" through "gain" phase**

9. **Openness is a dyadic relation**

10. **Difference between openness and inclusion**

11. **To survive a group needs personal ties**

12. **Compatibility**

1.   Sequence is Temporal

While the interpersonal need dimensions of inclusion, control and openness occur, in that order, in the development of the group, the sequence is a temporal one. As a group gets underway these interpersonal need areas get dealt with at a higher level and in a shorter span of time. For example, in a group where members are previously acquainted with each other, inclusion may proceed more swiftly than in a group of complete strangers. Nonetheless, despite its temporal nature the sequence follows the same developmental pattern of inclusion, control, and openness. The nature of group life is such that individuals on entering a group first focus on how to gain membership (inclusion), then focus on how much influence they want to exert and receive from others (control), and lastly on how much closeness they wish to experience with others (openness).

Schutz (1966) recounts how he once interviewed a participant who had just completed a thirty-meeting training group. In response to his question on how would she describe what happened in the group, the participant replied, "Well, first you're concerned about the problem of where you fit in the group; then you're wondering about what you will accomplish. Finally, after a while, you learn that people mean something" (p. 169).

2.   Phases are Not Distinct

These three phases of inclusion, control and openness are not distinct but interpersonal need areas that are emphasized and varying intensity at different points in a group's development. However, while all three areas are always present in a group they are not always of equal salience. For example, in the inclusion phase while the predominant focus is on belonging and entry into the group, members may touch on control and openness issues. In other words it would not be unusual for group members during this inclusion period to wonder about and observe what lies ahead. Thoughts such as "next time I'll suggest a better way of doing this activity" (control) and "I wonder if I will become friends with anyone here" (openness) are not uncommon.

However, as these needs are not of foremost importance during entry into a group, they recede into the background and what gets played out and emphasized is the central issue in the group. In this case since the central issue is one of gaining inclusion into the group, it would not be unusual for group members to think, "well, I might as well go along with what is happening in the group, for I want the group to like me," yet at the same time wonder what price it will take to be "in" and whether the rewards are worth the effort. These dynamics get compounded when an individual's unresolved need area begins to influence the group's preoccupation and work level.

3.   Phases are Not Always Reached or Completed

It is important to note that while this theory suggests that groups progress through inclusion and move on to control and openness, this does not necessarily mean that all groups are able to go through all of these phase. Firstly, not all groups meet long enough to experience all these phases, and secondly, groups, like people, can become immobilized at certain need levels and never go beyond a particular phase. For example, an individual who is overly conflicted in a particular need area can drag the group back to a particular phase. We also note that open-ended groups where membership is not fixed (e.g., patient groups in hospitals where members regularly leave and new ones frequently come in), often find it hard to move past the inclusion phase. In some cases when they do go past the inclusion phase into the control phase, the group gets dragged backed into the inclusion phase as new members enter.

While groups can get stuck at any phase, typically they get stuck at the control phase. It is most unfortunate when this happens, since it leaves group members with distaste and even fear of groups. In addition, this premature closure means the group has been unable to experience the insights and learnings that are derived from having adequately resolved this phase. For example, over the years I have noticed that some of my classes which were studying group development at the University have ended the course at the control phase either because of unresolved issues among group members or failure to resolve issues of authority. These issues get carried into the next group experience creating conflicted and unresolved need areas that will influence entry into that group.

Figure Ground Concept Illustrating a Group's Preoccupation with Inclusion, Control and Openness Needs

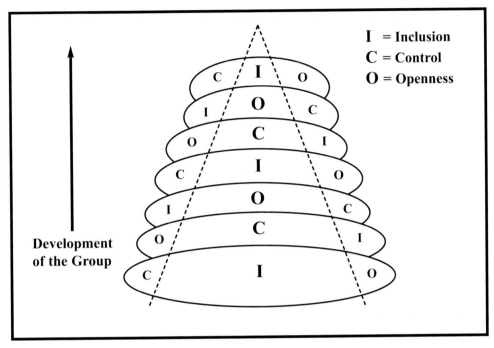

FIGURE IV-15
Adapted from Dimock, 1987.

The above diagram illustrates the background, foreground phenomena of the three interpersonal need areas. While all three dimensions are always present in the group's development they are not always of equal importance.

4.   Dimensions Get Revisited and Recycled

From Schutz's perspective, group formation is a process not limited to the initial coming together of a group. A group evolves through a sequence of area concerns requiring that each previous area be in operation before it can be worked on or at least partially resolved before it can proceed on to the next dimension. After a group is underway it moves from dimension to dimension as problems come up (Dimock, 1987).

Schutz uses the analogy of a mechanic tightening a wheel to illustrate this point:

> When a person changes a tire and replaces the wheel, he first sets the wheel in place and secures it by sequentially tightening each bolt, but just enough to keep the wheel in place and make the next step possible. Then the bolts are tightened farther, usually in the same sequence, until the wheel is firmly in place... In a similar way to the bolts, the need areas are worked on until they are handled satisfactorily enough to continue with the work at hand. Later on they are returned to and worked over to a more satisfactory degree. If one bolt was not tightened well on the first sequence, on the next cycle it must receive more attention, and so on (Schutz, 1966, p.172).

As these interpersonal need areas of inclusion, control and openness get resolved by the group it moves the development of that particular need area further along. Thus, with time, these areas get dealt with at a greater depth or more sophisticated level and in a shorter span of time. For example in the early period of a control phase, group members are quite preoccupied with how much influence they can exert on the group. Most of their energy goes into positioning themselves in the group. As the group evolves, these same group members, while still remaining interested in influencing the group, become aware of the importance of hearing from the others and of wanting to hear what they have to say. Still later, group members find themselves not only wanting to hear from others but they actively elicit opposing opinions, and solicit information as they recognize the different abilities and skills that exist in the group. All three illustrations cover the control phase however each illustration depicts the group dealing with this interpersonal need area in a progressively more mature manner.

This pattern of "formation and reformation" occurs whenever the group approaches a new meeting and or a new decision. Beebe & Materson (2000) give an interesting illustration to describe these patterns:

> If this process can be visualized, it might look something akin to a large jellyfish moving through the water. The jellyfish floats in the water in a relatively disorganized state until it needs to move forward: then it organizes itself, contracts, and propels itself through the water until it returns to a restful, less organized state. Group process moves through a similar series of contractions until it reaches its ultimate goal" (Beebe & Materson, 2000, pp.57-58).

5.   Reversal and Retracing of the Cycle

As a group nears closure the recycling of interpersonal needs shifts in sequence from inclusion, control and openness to openness, control and inclusion. Hence the final issue faced by the group will be the breaking up of the group and parting from friends. This is an interesting and well documented phenomenon. The openness and richness experienced in the end phases of a group leaves a good feeling with members. Friendships have been forged, good will has been exchanged and quality decisions have been made. The need to maintain and develop further dialogue and influence with various members (control) is a natural developmental need given the quality and circumstances of the context experienced.

This reversal in sequence as the group retraces its passage from openness through control to inclusion (O-C-I) can be observed by the almost ritualistic desire of group members to give feedback to one another before parting (openness), followed by detailed discussion as to why resistance or compliance of certain decisions had taken place and where the group had become blocked (control). Lastly, recognition by the group that members are dispersing in different directions is often followed by exchange of possibilities of continuing the group, e.g., having a reunion party. The end result of ensuring further contact via exchange of e-mail addresses and telephone numbers (inclusion) is a natural and direct by-product of the dialogue experienced by members in this openness phase.

6.   Individual versus Group

The question often arises as to the percentage of numbers (members) necessary to shift a group to another phase or maintain a group within its particular phase. The answer is not always clear. Often an individual's unresolved need area can make it impossible for the group to proceed further thus influencing a group's preoccupation with a particular phase. Concomitantly, an individual who is overly conflicted in a particular need area can drag a group back into a particular phase. Schutz (1966) suggests that "for certain individuals, a particular problem area will be so personally potent that it will transcend the current group issue." Thus an individual's "skewness" toward a particular need area can influence the life and growth of a group. The extent of the unresolved need and the rigidity with which it is dealt by all those concerned often determines the level and possibility of its resolution.

These unresolved needs often become more evident in the middle phase of the group where control issues of influence are being played out by a few individuals and where power struggles begin to be the order of the day. The impact of these unresolved issues influences the quality of and commitment to decisions made. If these issues continue to remain unresolved, they can stunt both the group's and the members' growth and lower the group's investment to its stated goals.

7.   Importance of the Inclusion Phase

One cannot underscore sufficiently the importance of the inclusion phase in Schutz's model of basic interpersonal needs. The maintenance and attention paid to the optimal achievement of this initial interpersonal need, is key to the success and further development of any group. When inclusion needs are not met, control needs often emerge in a dysfunctional and hostile manner. If control needs are not resolved and power issues dominate and colour the work, the group that has not resolved problems of membership is unlikely to develop much in the area of openness. As we can see "beginnings" not only influence the middle phases of a group but also the quality and possibility of a group's reaching the maturity level so necessary for a healthy termination to take place.

8.   The "Gain" Through "Pain" Phase

While the control phase is characterized by tremendous stress and tension it also holds the key to enormous learning and growth at the group and personal level. In other words this control phase is a necessary albeit painful requirement for the group's development. This period in a group's life cannot be underscored enough since most of us enter interpersonal and group relations with "unfinished" control issues characterized by questions such as, "how much do I want to influence?" and "how much do I want to be influenced?"

Variations of this basic theme get played out as facades drop and individuals establish personal roles, revealing more characteristic behaviours. It is during this period of turmoil, that underlying issues of power, authority and trust surface, the resolution of which paves the way for healthy development in the area of intimacy, affection and openness.

9.   Openness is a Dyadic Relation

Unlike inclusion and control, the dimension of openness can only occur between pairs of people. This is sometimes hard to grasp because the overall feeling in the group during this phase is one of warmth, trust and togetherness. The natural assumption is that the "good" feeling in the atmosphere is solely connected to the deep feelings members have towards the group as a whole. This is not so, for while good feelings do exist in the group as a whole, the heightened emotional feeling characteristic of this phase is quite different. The close personal feelings of "affectional" exchange of initiating and receiving openness described here can only exist and be felt between two people. This pairing off phenomena happens within the group context for the betterment of the group as opposed to the development of subgroups that tend to polarize or divide the group. These "affectional" exchanges get played out openly and naturally and are experienced by members as a non-exclusive activity.

10. Difference between Openness and Inclusion

It is interesting to note the difference between these two dimensions. The word "connect" conveys the surface nature of inclusion, whereas "authenticity" conveys the depth nature of openness. Inclusion has to do with formation, entry, the desire to connect, the wish to be a part of something and most importantly the need to be accepted by the group. The central concern is the acceptance of the individual by the group and the perception as to whether one is "in" or "out" of the group. The desired association here is emotionally superficial and undifferentiated. The aim here is to belong, to be acknowledged, and to be included; nothing more, nothing less.

With openness on the other hand, the desired association is emotionally deep and differentiated. The experience is a dyadic one and is generally built on the qualitative experiences inclusion and control. It also has a more mature dimension since it involves initiating and receiving feedback, responsibility-taking, influence and authenticity concerning the purposes of the group.

Because openness is based on the building of emotional ties, it is dependent on some form of inclusion activity, whereas inclusion, by virtue of the fact that it is the earliest interpersonal need in the life of the group, is independent of the openness dimension. Both, however, are necessary dimensions for healthy group development.

11. To Survive a Group Needs Personal Ties

In order for a group to survive and function effectively it needs the existence of personal ties among members. These ties become all the more important when the group has a task to accomplish which arouses member feelings or requires working closely together. Unless the group has developed the ability to handle feelings and emotions and is given enough freedom to have these expressed among members, productivity suffers because of the tie-up of energy in the suppression of hostile impulses. In addition, rivalries build, commitment wanes, misunderstandings develop, members sabotage the group, others leave the group, and the group life is over. Thus, it is the "human factors" which determine productivity and work group success, e.g., high morale and low absenteeism. Crucial to the survival of the group is either establishment of personal benefits or the development of "affectional" bonds through sharing and openness so critical to human relationships - including relationships at work, in service organizations, and in so-called non-intimate settings (Wilson, 1996).

12. Compatibility

Schutz (1955, 1966, 1989, 1992) has conducted research showing that groups comprised of members who are compatible in the areas of inclusion, control and openness are more likely to get along together, be productive and work on problems far more efficiently (Forsyth, 1999) than those that are not. The basis for this compatibility seems to be the orientation group members have towards interpersonal relations and how they have become accustomed to interacting with others. This would suggest for example that members who do not wish to control the group are more likely to get along together and be productive, than groups in which everyone wants to take on leadership and be in charge or no one wants to take on responsibility or make decisions. Incompatibility in the areas of inclusion and openness will have similar effect.

Schutz makes a distinction between "wanted behaviour" and "expressed behaviour" for each phase. These categories signify the degree of passivity or activity of an individual's behaviour in relation to getting interpersonal satisfaction in the group in any given area (Forsyth, 1999). Compatibility, then is measured both as the "dimension of the need and in the way the need is handled" (Durkin, 1964).

Schutz (1984) states that compatibility is not static and that groups and individuals evolve over time and can change their modus operandi to become more effective. Thus compatibility and relationship development are always changeable. The strategic determinant of compatibility is the particular blend of orientation towards authority and towards personal intimacy, openness and interpersonal considerations (Schutz, 1955, Bennis, 1964).

In his book "The Truth Option" Schutz (1984) discusses the importance of "atmosphere compatibility" within which relationships occur. He writes "when you and I prefer the same atmosphere (or climate or context) we have a common basis on which to resolve issues." He goes on to add that "atmosphere incompatibility results from disagreement about the basis for resolving differences, not from the differences themselves" (Schutz, 1984, p. 195). For example the climate in a group would become quite charged if some members want an issue to be "talked through" while others want to "work it out individually." Some want to "plan and use structure" whereas others want to "go with the flow." Still others want to "put the cards on the table" while others may want to "be discreet and judicious" (Schutz, 1984, p.198).

Another area of compatibility that Schutz discusses is that of "role compatibility" where opposites attract. His discussion sheds light as to why alliances and sub-groupings develop in groups. These differences in orientation (compatibility/incompatibility) are further described in the following way. For example, if I want to control you and you want to be controlled, we would get along well. However, if we both wish to control, we would have a "competitive incompatibility," whereas, if "we both prefer to be controlled, we are in danger of being incompatible due to apathy" (Schutz 1984, p.230, Schutz, 1992).

There is also a relationship between compatibility and productivity. Schutz (1955, 1984) states that the C-P effect[3] varies with the task and increases with time pressure. His studies indicate that "under time pressure, compatible groups perform even better than they do without pressure, while incompatible groups become more ineffective" (Schutz, 1984, p. 243). One of the reasons why this is true is that when a group is 'rushed' under time pressure, there is a suspension (of sorts) of maintenance behaviours such as checking and clarifying. These maintenance behaviours allow for incompatibility to be worked out. Without the time pressure, these efforts to smooth out relations are not performed, leading to blocks in communication and bad feelings. Therefore compatibility is particularly relevant when the group is 'under the gun'.

---

[3] The effect of compatibility on productivity.

Similarities and Differences

Key Points

1. Inclusion is primarily concerned with the formation of relations, whereas control and openness are concerned with relations already formed.

2. In an argument, the inclusion seeker wants to join in, whereas the control seeker wants to win.

3. Control behaviour differs from openness behaviour in that it has to do with power relations whereas openness has to do with authentic relations.

4. For inclusion and openness, there is a tendency for members to act similarly in both the behaviour they express and want from others, whereas in the control dimension, those who like to control do not necessarily want others to control them.

5. Inclusion and openness differ in that in inclusion there is a general interest in people although not in particular individuals, whereas in the openness mode interest is directed to particular persons, involves strong emotional attachments and is dyadic.

FIGURE IV-16

PERSONAL NOTES ON SCHUTZ

REFERENCES

Beebe, S.A. & Masterson, J.T. (2000). *Communicating in small groups* (6*th* ed.). New York: Addison Wesley Longman, Inc.

Bennis, W.G. (1964). Patterns and vicissitudes in T-group development. In L.D. Bradford, J.R. Gibb, & K.D. Benne, (Eds), *T-Group theory and laboratory method.* New York: John Wiley and Sons, Inc. (pp. 248-278).

Cartwright, D. & Zander, A. (1968). Group dynamics: Research and theory (3*rd* ed.). New York: Harper & Row.

Cragan, J.F. & Wright, D.W. (1999). *Communicating in small groups.* Boston: Wadsworth Publishing Co.

Dimock, H.G. & Devine, I. (1996). *Managing dynamic groups* (3*rd* ed.). North York, ON: Captus Press Inc.

Dimock, H.G. (1987). *Groups: Leadership and group development.* San Diego: University Associates, Inc.

Dimock, H.G. (1967). *Individual growth and organizational effectiveness: Part 1 - Individual growth.* Unpublished paper, Montreal: Sir George Williams University.

Durkin, H.E. (1964). *The group in depth.* New York: International Universities Press Inc.

Forsyth, D.R. (1999). *Group dynamics (3rd ed.).* Boston: Wadsworth Publishing Inc.

Hare, A.P. (1976). *Handbook of small group processes (2nd ed.).* New York: Free Press.

Liberman, M.A., Yalom, J.D. & Miles, M.B. (1973). *Encounter groups: First facts.* New York: Basic Books.

Napier, R.W. & Gershenfeld, M.K. (1999). *Groups: Theory and practice (6th ed.).* Boston: Houghton Mifflin Company.

Scaffer, J.B. & Zalinsky, M.D. (1974). *Models of group therapy and sensitivity training.* New Jersey: Prentice-Hall, Inc.

Schutz, W.C. (1989). *The interpersonal underworld.* Mill Valley, CA: Will Schutz & Associates.

Schutz, W.C. (1984). *The truth option*. Berkley, CA: Ten Speed Press.

Schutz, W.C. (1982). *Profound simplicity.* San Diego: University Associates, Inc.

Schutz, W.C. (1966). *FIRO - A three dimensional theory of behaviour.* Reprinted as T*he interpersonal underworld*. Palo Alto, CA: Science and Behaviour Books.

Schutz, W.C. (1955). *What makes groups effective.* Human Relations, 8, 429-465.

Shaw, M. (1981). *Group dynamics: The psychology of small group behaviour.* New York: McGraw-Hill.

Waterman, J.A. & Rogers, J. (1996). *Introduction to the FIRO - B.* Palo Alto, CA: Consulting Psychologists Press, Inc.

Wheelan, S. (1994). *Group processes: A developmental perspective.* Toronto: Allyn and Bacon.

Wilson, G.L. (1996). *Groups in context (4th ed.).* New York: McGraw Hill, Inc.

V. TUCKMAN'S DEVELOPMENTAL SEQUENCE IN SMALL GROUPS

OVERVIEW

In 1965, Tuckman reviewed fifty-five articles dealing with stages of group development in order to look at the question of **change in process over time.** These reviews are based on studies from four fields: therapy groups, human relations training groups, laboratory-task groups, and natural groups. From these studies, he abstracted four stages of group development which he called: **forming, storming, norming**, and **performing;** he later added a fifth stage: **adjourning** (Tuckman and Jensen, 1977). The addition of this fifth stage reflects the more recent research in group development that suggests the existence of a distinct and final stage in the life of a group.

While Tuckman's reviews are based on studies in four fields, it is important to note that certain settings were over-represented, e.g., group therapy settings, while others under-represented, e.g., the laboratory-task group and natural settings. In addition to the inequality of setting representation, Tuckman's original framework was first abstracted from the over-represented sample of group therapy studies, later to be applied to human relations training groups and still later to laboratory-task and natural groups. These limitations necessitate caution in considering his theory as truly representative of developmental stages in groups of all types. While his suggested sequence and perceptions of trends appeared to hold under varied conditions of composition, size, duration and focus, and while Tuckman's theory would seem to stand the test of common sense, generalizations must perforce be limited to the fact that what has been put forth is mainly delineated from research dealing with group therapy settings.

Tuckman summarized the result of his studies into a five stage model, concluding that groups pass through a developmental sequence of change. Each of these stages is seen as unique but not separate or disconnected from the next, in that, unresolved concerns in one stage weigh heavily in the next, influencing the ability of the group to move on constructively. This is a sequential model which appears in a specific order, occurring naturally but without a set time frame.

→ might not go through all of them, & might not be in order

The **five stages** which Tuckman formulated from his comprehensive summarization of small group research are described as follows:

Stage I **Forming:** Members become oriented to each other and the task at hand.
(fitting in) Dependency on leader and testing of behaviour appear.

Stage II **Storming:** Members find themselves in conflict, the management of which
(Role) becomes the focus. Antagonism and turmoil appear.

Stage III **Norming:** Rules of behaviour appropriate to the group and necessary for
the task are spelled out. Period of cohesion and cooperation
(norms) appear.

Stage IV **Performing:** Group works as a unit to achieve goals and accomplish the task.
Emergence of solutions appears.

Stage V **Adjourning:** Termination of tasks and disengagement from relationships.
Group disbands.

Each of the five basic stages described are further divided into **two** realms of group behaviour. One related to the interpersonal and the other, to the work of the group. The realms related to the interpersonal are described under the category of **group structure**; they have to do with the way members interact and relate to one another in the group, i.e., the socio-emotional activities of a group. Those related to the work realms are described under the category of **task activity** and have to do with the work that has to be accomplished and the content of the interaction as it relates to the task, i.e., the instrumental or task oriented activities of a group. These two realms play a substantial role in the way each stage is resolved, with progress in one influencing the progress in the other.

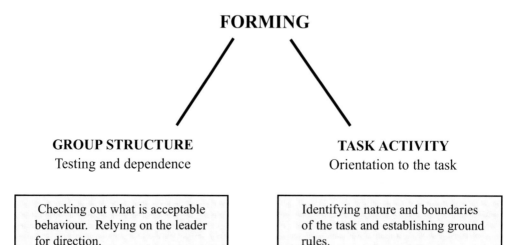

FORMING

GROUP STRUCTURE
Testing and dependence

TASK ACTIVITY
Orientation to the task

Checking out what is acceptable behaviour. Relying on the leader for direction.

Identifying nature and boundaries of the task and establishing ground rules.

Group Structure

As members get together for the first time, there is a period of uncertainty, caution and anxiety as they try to determine their place in the group as well as the procedures and rules of the group. Members discover the boundaries of the situation by testing what interpersonal behaviours are acceptable, based on the reactions of the leader and other group members. This initial caution of interpersonal exploration associated with any new experience, is an attempt by group members to play it safe and avoid rejection of others. Napier & Gershanfeld (1981) suggest that "forming" incorporates all of the discomfort and awkwardness found in any new situation where "one's ego is involved in new relationships," hence preoccupation with the "oughts," "shoulds," and "what ifs" of the situation.

This initial period of orientation and testing is characterized by "hesitant participation" (Corsini, 1957), "tentative interaction" (Maples, 1988), and self-consciousness. Polite discourse prevails as members camouflage their feelings and put on a facade. During this stage, individuals test their compatibility for being there against the stated reasons of other members. The accompanying anxiety often stems from an awareness of differences in styles or needs, and a concern over ambiguity. This often results in a quick acceptance of structure and arbitrary norms.

The intra-psychic pressure that comes to bear on the group during this formation stage, is a powerful influence of preset notions that members first have as they enter the group, of what it will or should be like. Berne (1963) refers to this as the unique formation of each individual's "group imago." These mental pictures, which are based on previous group experiences, emerge as expectations and act as filters through which early interaction takes place. Unless these expectations are adjusted to meet the reality of the group situation, the individual is bound to have difficulties contributing to the task and remaining committed to the goals of the group. These difficulties spill into the interpersonal realm, limiting the individual's ability to engage effectively with others, thus hindering the development of the group.

In some groups where participation is compulsory, forced or involuntary, e.g., hospitalized narcotic addicts, court ordered delinquent supervision, or compulsory course requirements at college or university, the initial stage of testing-dependence is preceded by a pre-stage of "unshared behaviour" (Martin & Hill, 1957) characterized by resistance, silence and hostility.

The forming stage is characterized by strong expression of dependency on the leader, or other high status members, for direction and clarification of the goals and the procedures of the group. In fact, the tendency is to assume that the leader will provide all the structure, set the ground rules, establish the agenda, and do all the leading. Leaders, who do not conform to this expectation, often intensify the frustration and anxiety within the group.

This predominant feature of dependency is further characterized by members looking to the leader for support, guidance, and permission. This often extends beyond the leader to powerful members and existing norms such as who gets to decide what, or pre-existing standards, such as productivity expectations. In interdisciplinary teams seen in hospital settings, where professionals who represent different fields frequently sit on the same committee, (nurse, doctor, physiotherapist, speech therapist, occupational therapist, etc.), members show high dependency on the role relationships developed outside of the group and on the fixed hierarchy of responsibilities that accompany their roles. The dependency on role to determine power boundaries within the team, not only plays an important role in reducing anxiety and ambiguity, it also influences member contribution, often fostering the development of submission.

Task Activity

As members enter a new group, the task and its underlying focus looms high in their minds. Quite early in the session, members attempt to identify the nature and boundaries of the task, and the manner in which the group experience will be used to accomplish it. Questions such as: "What are we supposed to do?" and "To whom are we responsible?" are raised. Depending on the setting and nature of the group, questions related to time frames, resources, accountability and exchange of functional information begin to surface. What is important to note, is that in orienting to the task, members are essentially defining it by discovering its ground rules.

Where the task is to develop how to learn, in regards to interpersonal sensitivity, i.e., the "process" of group formation versus a clear mandate given the group to do a job, the interpersonal/task distinction becomes fuzzy, and clarity around the nature and boundaries of what one needs to accomplish becomes less clear. In other words, where the task becomes the "process," the very existence of ambiguity becomes central to the group's development. As members wrestle with establishing ground rules, and search for structure to accomplish the task, it begins to be accomplished.

Discussion during this stage wavers between relevant and irrelevant issues. Griping with the institutional environment (hostile comments about the institution's inability to set priorities), intellectualization (expounding on the work and importance of groups), and discussion of peripheral problems (gossiping about an absent membe's life style) are some of the indirect ways of approaching orientation. More direct attempts at orientation are observed as members endeavour to define the task or determine the approach to be used. Other examples are the attempts to exchange relevant information and identify resources that are available in the group.

The forming stage ends as the group settles down to work individually and collectively. Bonds of similarity begin to emerge and members begin to relax.

Summary of Trends and Activities during the Forming Stage

Group Development Stage	Group Structure	Task Activity	Feelings Generated	Need Level	Desired Outcome
Forming	Testing of acceptable behaviour Dependence on leader for direction	Orientation to defining the task and establishing ground rules	Anxiety Confusion Curiosity Enthusiasm Low tolerance for ambiguity Let down Politeness Concern	Physiological safety Security	Commitment Acceptance

FIGURE V-1

123

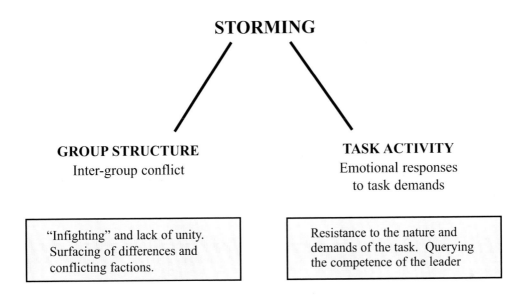

STORMING

GROUP STRUCTURE
Inter-group conflict

TASK ACTIVITY
Emotional responses
to task demands

"Infighting" and lack of unity.
Surfacing of differences and
conflicting factions.

Resistance to the nature and
demands of the task. Querying
the competence of the leader

Group Structure

Anxiety, threat and resistance characterize this stage with members becoming annoyed, irritated, or hostile toward one another and toward the leader "as a means of expressing their individuality and resisting the formation of the group structure" (Hare, 1982). Resistance from members is "multi-directed" and aimed at the task, the discussion at hand, the leader, other group members, or the group in general, with members becoming increasingly more anxious and less cautious in their interaction with one another (Gladding, 1991).

The bonds of similarity, which began to emerge during the previous stage, rapidly give way to sharp differences that revolve around issues of group structure, task direction and interpersonal relationships. These issues ultimately polarize group opinion resulting in the formation of factions. The essence of the struggle boils down to conflict over "progressing" into the unknown of interpersonal relations (intimacy) or "regressing" to the security of earlier dependence (Tuckman, 1965). Warring factions representing each side of the polarized issue emerge: those favouring playing it safe versus risk-taking, those inclined to be more active versus passive, those desiring to stay with the familiar versus those anxious to experiment, and those who are task oriented versus those who are socio-emotional. The polarization represents a return to the security of earlier dependence (Kelman, 1980), for by so doing, members remain dependent, in that they are not "initiating" any activity but rather reacting to the events that are unfolding. These events or critical incidents result in the emergence of a group leader, thus further intensifying the dependence, albeit temporary.

Interaction during this period is typified by disruptive communication, nitpicking, bickering, negative comments, judgements, criticisms, and in-fighting. This stage is further characterized by sharp fluctuation of feelings (elated versus frustrated, optimistic versus pessimistic, etc.), brief but intense "brittle linkages" between members (Powdermaker & Frank, 1948), backtracking of relationships, rivalry, animosity and the formation of conflicting factions. It is important to note that storming does not always involve acts of aggression; it sometimes is characterized by apathy, passivity, disinterest and lack of energy in group members. In such situations, there has probably been insufficient forming (Clarkson, 1991).

What is outstanding in this stage is the glaring lack of unity. Parker (1958) refers to this stage as a "crisis period." Weber (1982), who sees this as the most difficult stage of development to tolerate, refers to this period as a "maze" of frustrating cycles of reaction from which the group needs to break out. (Mann, 1953) describes this as a period of hostility punctured by "disruption" and "fragmentation."

This difficult stage is viewed by some as a "distraction" and by others as a stage to be avoided. However, it is also a very productive one, for as the group works out its "threshold of tension" (Gladding, 1991), this storming period provides an arena for group members to work through issues of power and control, essential skills for the group's future. In addition, the "infighting" and lack of unity experienced in this stage provide the basis for future development of interdependent behaviour amongst members - an impossible task to achieve unless issues of conflict have been acknowledged and dealt with as a group.

Task Activity

Emotional response to the task varies greatly between settings, and it is dependent on the focus and goal of the group. In therapy or human relations training groups, where the task is the "process" of group formation and where the focus is self-understanding or personal development, the emotional response to the task takes on a form of extreme resistance. This is particularly evident when the behaviour demanded by the task is in direct contradiction to the individual's inclination. In such situations resistive behaviours are typified by the following: questioning of the authority figure and the validity of the approach being used, challenging the timing and appropriateness of the material being presented, displaying anger at the uncovering of conflict, and deflecting any facilitation directed toward the reason of the group's existence.

In natural settings of professional groups (i.e., business, medical, education, etc.) and laboratory task groups, where committees and project groups are struck up to complete a task, the intense emotionality described earlier is less visible as the task is unrelated to the examination of self at a "penetrating level" (Tuckman, 1965) and is directly non-threatening in nature. Nonetheless, emotionality does exist in the form of task related issues: e.g., decisions as to work rules and procedures, responsibility, testing of feasibility of proposals presented, nitpicking, putting down of suggestions and ignoring members who seem to have lower status.

This emotionality can appear in the form of an "illusion of work" in which members, while seemingly focused on the task at hand, are in reality using the activity to jockey for position as the pecking order begins to get established.

While storming ostensibly appears to be about the nature and demands of the task, in reality, it is about the perceived competence of the leader and her/his ability to survive members taking over. In all settings, this is a stressful period for both group members and the leader. No matter how clear the task or structure of the group, or how reasonable the demands of the situation, or how appropriate the interventions of the leader, the emotional response of resistance to the task seems to be a necessary precursor to the solid and creative work the group eventually begins to engage in.

Some groups become "arrested" in this storming stage by falling into the trap of either "dwelling" on the conflict or "ignoring" it. What is evident is that the greater awareness the group has of what it has been able to work through, the better position it is in to move on and do its work.

Summary of Trends and Activities during the Storming Stage

Group Development Stage	Group Structure	Task Activity	Feelings Generated	Need Level	Desired Outcome
Storming	"Infighting" and lack of unity Surfacing of conflicting factions	Resistance to the nature and demands of the task Querying competence of the leader	Hurt Resistance Fear Hostility Negativity Rebellion Animosity	Belonging Social	Clarification Awareness Belonging

FIGURE V-2

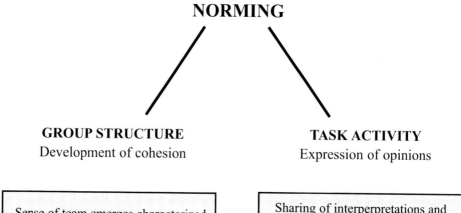

NORMING

GROUP STRUCTURE	TASK ACTIVITY
Development of cohesion	Expression of opinions
Sense of team emerges characterized by " group spirit."	Sharing of interperpretations and perspectives. Openness of members to each other.

Group Structure

With the tensions and frustrations of the last stage behind them, the group enters a period of settling down and pulling together, where cohesion, collaboration, and mutual support prevail. This stage is characterized by a strong sense of "we'ness," in-group consciousness where members become more sensitive and conscious of each other as a group with a sense of camaraderie and "group spirit." During this period, development of group structure and the process of norming become a central focus. The norms, or agreed upon values that develop, not only help to regulate members' behaviours and ensure the group's existence, but also set the pattern for the next stage.

The group, desirous of a new and harmonious culture, engages in a "patching-up" process in which norms and values peculiar to the group emerge. The establishment of new group-generated norms to ensure its existence contribute to the reduction of conflict, and the resolution of polarized issues evident in the storming stage. We also note that the discrepancy experienced between "what is and what is needed" begins to disappear. This stage marks the development of norms that support openness (Bradford, 1964a), member responsibility (Barron & Krulee, 1948), and mutuality, the maintenance of interpersonal relationships, solidarity, and freedom in communication.

In therapy or human relations training groups, the new norms that evolve and the new roles adopted, usher in an era in which members feel valued, supported, listened to, and acknowledged. The mood is such that a sense of loyalty to the group develops with members becoming invested in its future. The development of "we consciousness" (Abrahams, 1949) and the emergence of mutual involvement between members, provide a powerful unifying force to both the group and the task at hand.

In laboratory-task settings or "natural groups" where the focus is primarily directed toward task accomplishment, we see the establishment of norms that regulate the functioning of the group as a unit. As members shift from an "individualistic" goal orientation to a "cooperative" and interdependent one (Tuckman, 1991), collaboration increases, and with it a sense of team spirit. This achievement of interdependence through the resolution of differences, signals a significant shift in the development and maturity of the group.

Task Activity

Given the new structure and culture generated by the norms in the early part of this stage, the challenge the group now faces, is putting it into good use. Having attained harmony, the group enters into a phase where members try to maintain it at all costs. In an endeavour to ensure that this harmony prevails, the group avoids any form of task conflict resulting in "smooth relations" and periods of enchantment.

During this period, openness to the task at hand facilitates the working through of differences in goal orientation. This is particularly evident in educational groups, where students shift from a competitive mode of goal orientation of "seeking not only to succeed but to make other students fail" (Tuckman, 1991), to a more interdependent one of exchange of information, sharing of facts and learning from each other. What is also observed during this stage is openness of members to each other and a growing respect for individual differences. This enables recognition of individual talent and the healthy use of available resources. This process paves the way for consensus-seeking in decision-making and agreement on rules. Time limits and parameters of what needs to be done is addressed and new approaches discussed. "Information gets acted upon" (Tuckman, 1965), a sense of flow takes place and brief periods of playfulness are experienced. Corporate responsibility for the group and feelings of enthusiasm about the work being done and about each member's role in it infuse the group.

In therapy or human relations training groups where self and other group members are the basic inputs, task opinions involve statements about self and others. The task of self-exploration begins to get accomplished as personal opinions are freely expressed, and as members begin to exchange relevant interpretations about what has transpired. Probing and revealing at a highly intimate level and discussing and exploring personal data in a deeper manner, follow. Giving and receiving feedback plays a key role, as this is a time when group members are "available for insight" (Clarkson, 1991), growth and action.

In professional and laboratory-task groupings, where task accomplishment of a less personal nature is expected, exploring of actions related to the task, defining the problem, giving and receiving of opinions and exchanging of relevant information, facilitate member involvement. While emotionality still runs high, it is of a constructive nature, for it contributes to the basic task at hand. As group members get more informed and as resources get used in a more balanced way, shared decision-making and problem-solving, resulting in quality work, begin to emerge.

Cohesion is seen as the "last stage in the interpersonal process of norming" (Gladding, 1991). It plays an important role in trust building, feelings of solidarity, and sense of commitment and involvement. It is at this stage that the group becomes efficient, capable and productive. On the other hand, the inherent danger of a cohesive structure is not always visible (Kellerman, 1981). The danger resides in the tyranny and influence, the group can now exert on its members to "tow the line," and execute the group's wishes. Depending on its punitive structure and motivational attitudes behind them, this stage of "group think" or "group mind set" can also be used in destructive and unhealthy ways.

Summary of Trends and Activities during the Norming Stage

Group Development Stage	Group Structure	Task Activity	Feelings Generated	Need Level	Desired Outcome
Norming	Sense of team emerges characterized by "group spirit"	Sharing of interpretations and perspectives. Openness of members to each other.	Warmth Excitement Trust Enchantment Affection	Recognition Self-esteem	Involvement Support Loyalty Mutual respect

FIGURE V-3

129

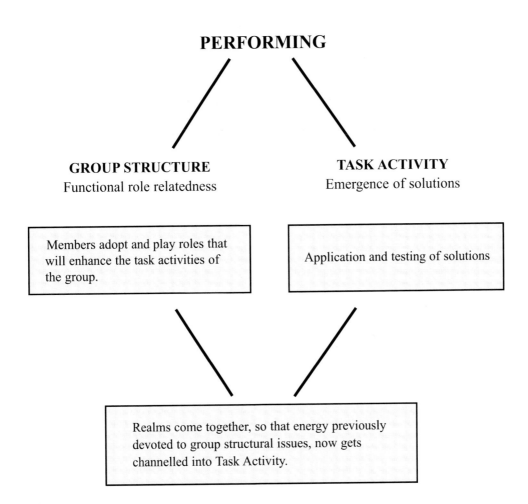

PERFORMING

GROUP STRUCTURE
Functional role relatedness

TASK ACTIVITY
Emergence of solutions

Members adopt and play roles that will enhance the task activities of the group.

Application and testing of solutions

Realms come together, so that energy previously devoted to group structural issues, now gets channelled into Task Activity.

Group Structure

This is a special and productive stage in which the interpersonal structures of the group enter into full service of the task activity. With structural issues related to "membership, orientation, leadership and roles" (Napier & Gershanfeld, 1981) having been resolved, the group can now focus its energy into task accomplishment. The group is now free to develop "working alternatives" with "minimum emotional interaction," (Hare, 1982) and "minimum interference from distracting group processes" (Clarkson, 1991), such as getting off the subject, coming back to the same "dead" issue, whispering to others, or leaving the room, etc. Thus, the group becomes a problem-solving instrument, and enters into action stage culminating in work that is impressive.

The general atmosphere in the group is one of support and openness, with deep personal concern shown on a consistent level for and to each other. Members are now able to work on "individual and group goals" (Gladding, 1991) in a constructive and responsible manner. As the group becomes a sounding board, off which the work gets played out, members adopt meaningful and functional roles. These roles are not an issue but a means to accomplish the task and thus become a vehicle through which solid work gets achieved and integrated. This positive interdependence among members permits an interplay and flexibility in the roles, that allow for "leading when appropriate and following when productive and necessary" (Weber, 1982).

In therapy or human relations training groups, there is a high visibility of task function and mutual task interaction. The structure serves as a therapeutic function and supports rather than hinders the work at hand. Martin and Hill (1957) call this a period in which the group serves as an "integrative creative social instrument;" Mann (1953) refers to it as a period of "personal mutual synthesis." As the group provides support and opportunity to test out new and creative ways of doing things, "insight" leading to solution and action occurs. We note a work structure that permits the "use of differences" (Hearn, 1957) and the acceptance of each other. We also note "strong but flexible norms" (Bradford, 1964a) further contributing to the collaborative and productive work, typical of this stage.

In professional and laboratory-task settings, where the emphasis is on task achievement, we see the development of member responsibility and "heightened awareness of self and others" (Maples, 1988). Members are also able to express themselves without "censoring" their responses, resulting in "positive interdependence and mutuality" (Schroder & Harvey, 1963). We also note the emergence of role flexibility and role distribution, which further enhance the group's capacity to engage in situational leadership. As the group engages in effective problem-solving, it experiences autonomy and a high degree of satisfaction from the work it is able to produce. Thus, group structure has now become supportive of task performance.

Task Activity

The emphasis of this stage in the group's development is on attainment of the desired goal. Most of the energy during this period is directed toward constructive action leading to task accomplishment with activity completely overshadowing emotionality. The maturity of the group at this stage depends on its ability to permit the "development of interdependence of task goals and interpersonal relationships" (Napier & Gershanfeld, 1981). The trusting and comfortable atmosphere reflected in the functional roles adopted by group members permits the emergence of creative and insightful solutions. The group is now able to use its potential, and thus, is able to function with ease and efficiency, creating a basis or infrastructure for maximum outcome. We see the application of learnings, as well as the desire to contribute and facilitate the learnings of others.

In therapy or human relations training groups, as the group tackles its work, "consolidation" (Kellerman, 1981) of ideas begins to occur. Members work together with a minimum of emotional interaction. This does not in any way detract or lessen the mutual acceptance, support and deepening of communication experienced throughout the performing stage. A key feature during this period is that of the emergence of insight, and of personal and interpersonal constructive self-change made possible through responsible and "growthful feedback" (Egan, 1970). We see how members develop an understanding to internalize learning (Bradford, 1964b) and to generalize this learning to other situations.

In the professional realm, the group becomes a problem-solving instrument, directed to relevant task-related activities. In professional groups, there is an emphasis on evaluation of the group's product (Bales, 1950), assessment, and testing of feasibility of actions and proposals. The tasks are well defined (Kellerman, 1981), and roles such as giving and receiving of suggestions based on earlier information and evaluation, are freely offered by members in service of group problem-solving and decision making. We note that the group engages in creative inquiry, open discussion and "realistic appraisal of what could be accomplished" (Tuckman & Jensen, 1977). We also note, that task and maintenance roles become balanced, i.e., while highly task oriented it is also member oriented.

Performing is one of the most productive stages in group development, and tends to last longer, than any other stage mentioned earlier - an estimate of about 40-50% of the total group time (Maples, 1988).

Summary of Trends and Activities
during the Performance Stage

Group Development Stage	Group Structure	Task Activity	Feelings Generated	Need Level	Desired Outcome
Performing	Members adopt and play roles that will enhance the task activities of the group	Application and testing of solutions	Pride Satisfaction Autonomy	Achievement Self-actualization	Achievement Constructive use of differences. Application of learnings Collaborative problem-solving

FIGURE V-4

132

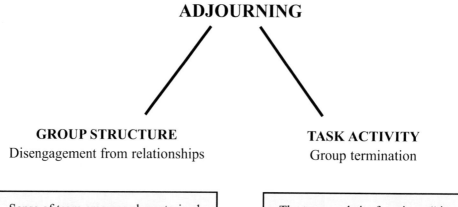

ADJOURNING

GROUP STRUCTURE
Disengagement from relationships

TASK ACTIVITY
Group termination

Sense of team emerges characterized by "group spirit."

The team ends its functions, "ties up loose ends" and disbands.

Group Structure

This stage has to do with closure. An important and often neglected part of group process. Closure occurs when the purpose of the group has been achieved, or when time for the group has ended. Here we note that the group's task has become that of disengagement from the relationships it has built up over time. The collective focus is directed toward the "divestment of emotional energy" (Clarkson, 1991) from the rich experience of group cohesion. The "hesitant participation" featured in the forming stage gives way to "reluctant action" (Maples, 1988) in the adjourning stage.

In therapy or human relations training groups, this disengagement process is often experienced with much intensity, regret, and increased emotionality. The pain and joy resulting from work done together, bond members to such an extent that it is not uncommon to attempt to escape the pain of disengagement by "denying" the actual benefits derived from the experience. On the whole, however, feelings of sadness give way to appreciation. Groups vary in how they deal with this process, with most having some structured time set aside for farewell rituals that are congruent with the group's norms. During this period, feedback is freely exchanged between members with a particular focus on experience and/or selected impact of some members. Nostalgia often sets in. Reluctance to leave is evident as last hugs and embraces are exchanged. Attempts to deny the inevitable ending of the group, is observed as members try to retain contact through plans of reunions, "annual get-togethers," etc. Failure to disengage and acknowledge that the group's purpose and life have truly ended leads to a "hollow unfinished feeling in the future" (Weber, 1982) influencing future formation in other groups. Clarkson (1991) suggests that the process of termination is often "deeper and more effective" if the group has been able to successfully deal with closure issues.

In professional and laboratory-task groups, the process of disengagement is usually experienced in more functional ways. The bonding observed through shared experiences of wrestling with the task sets the tone for "striking up" new and future work-related relations amongst some group members. Since the task, which originally brought the group together, was of a less personal nature, disengagement, while sometimes tinged with regret, is generally experienced more easily. In situations where there has been little to no task accomplishment in the performing stage, the process of disengagement is void of achievement and fulfilment with members viewing the prospect of termination with relief. We note that usually a brief set time frame with a clear end point is structured to recognize participation and achievement.

Task Activity

As the group ends its collective function, acknowledgement of task completion becomes a central focus. This acknowledgement takes different forms depending on the focus and setting of the group. In therapy, or human relations training groups, where the focus is self-understanding and personal development, termination takes place as members bring closure to their own experiences by acknowledging personal insights and the relevance of what they have learned to outside situations. During this period, members also engage in life review of the group. This nostalgic overview of events and their meaning while poignant, particularly, since the work was accomplished through group and interpersonal relationships, play an important role in bringing closure to the group and termination to the task.

In professional and laboratory-task groups, termination of task takes the form of "tying up of loose ends," highlighting accomplishments, assessing the quality of outcome, terminating duties, and acknowledging roles and contributions. As the group successfully achieves a full life cycle, it has no choice but to end. Ending may stir up mixed feelings; however, a mature group which has been able to meet both individual and group needs is aware of a mission accomplished and a task that has reached termination.

While accounts of the terminal phase of a group are relatively rare, it is generally felt that the timing and length of this process are critical. When too little time has been devoted to the process, the importance of closure is often obscured, whereas when extended, it can hinder disengagement and become counter-productive.

Summary of Trends and Activities
during the Adjourning Stage

5)

Group Development Stage	Group Structure	Task Activity	Feelings Generated	Need Level	Desired Outcome
Adjourning	Modes of disengagement from the team	The team ends its functions "ties up loose ends" and disbands	Sadness Nostalgia Regret Denial Appreciation Relief	Completion	Recognition Satisfaction Sense of achievement Insight Integration Fulfilment

FIGURE V-5

Key Characteristics and Useful Member Skills
During Each Stage

Group Development Stage	Key Characteristics	Useful Member Skills
Forming	• Hesitant participation • Exchange of functional information • Dependence on leader for direction • Discovering boundaries and appropriate parameters • Orientation toward others and the situation	• Getting acquainted, networking • Goal setting, identifying resources • Contracting, clarifying
Storming	• Multi-directed resistance • Formation of conflicting factions • Polarization of issues • Fluctuation of feelings • Lack of unity	• Perspective taking, assertiveness • Conflict management • Active listening, flexibility • Giving information • Giving opinions • Mediating-harmonizing
Norming	• Development of cohesive structure • Brief indulgence in playfulness • In-group consciousness • Acceptance of others and respect for individual differences • Establishment of roles and relationships	• Feedback, encouragement • Seeking opinions, giving opinions • Discernment, playfulness • Acceptance of differences • Defining the problem • Coordinating, exploring
Performing	• Task activity overshadows emotionality • Group becomes a sounding board off which task gets played out • Role flexibility and role distribution encourage situational leadership • Support and opportunity for experimentation and discovery • Development of interdependence of task goals and interpersonal relationships	• Decision making, problem-solving • Openness to new ideas • Role flexibility • Testing of feasibility • Supporting, encouraging • Following • Orienting, facilitating
Adjourning	• Nostalgic overview of events • Increased emotionality and disintegration • Expression of learnings and insights • Acknowledgement of roles and contributions • Termination of duties and responsibilities	• Letting go, evaluating • Reviewing • Linking activities to outside situations, celebrating • Coordinating, giving opinions • Defining the problem

FIGURE V-6

KEY FEATURES OF TUCKMAN'S THEORY

1. **Progressive linear model**

2. **Length and sequence of stages**

3. **How groups get stuck**

4. **Norms**

5. **Adjourning**

1.   Progressive Linear Model

This is a progressive linear model. Tuckman describes the group as moving from a hesitant testing stage through conflict and cohesion to task accomplishment. It is progressive in the sense that the group is portrayed as moving toward the resolution of distinct issues. It is linear in the sense that the group moves onward and upward toward the implicit goals of the group.

In some ways Tuckman's theory could be regarded as a life cycle model with the addition of Jensen's fifth stage (Tuckman & Jensen, 1977) of adjournment. The life cycle model emphasizes the termination phase of a group most pronounced in time-limited therapy, or training groups, where members show concern with a "return to the outside."

If this theory is looked at from a life cycle perspective, tracing the relationship between Tuckman's developmental stages and that of an individual's developmental cycle, reveals interesting parallels of a birth to death cycle. As in the development of the person, certain stages within the group are difficult and painful, while others are rich and fulfilling; still others are frustrating, yet exhilarating.

The Relationship Between a Group's Developmental Stages Compared to that of an Individual's Developmental Cycle

Stages	Group Life Cycle	Individual Life Cycle
I	Forming	Infancy
II	Storming	Adolescence
III	Norming Performing	Adulthood
IV	Adjourning	Generativity

FIGURE V-7

2.   Length and Sequence of Stages

Not all of Tuckman's stages last the same amount of time. Some groups move very quickly through the initial stages (forming, storming, and norming) spend considerable time in the performing stage and then move to terminating very quickly. Others linger interminably in the storming stage leaving little time for task accomplishment, thus influencing any sense of completion and satisfaction so critical in the adjourning stage.

Some of the variables influencing the time and length of each stage are: size, composition, nature of the group, style of leadership, culture, expectations, duration of group life, pre-history and history of the group, critical incidents, and compulsory or voluntary participation.

Movement from stage to stage can be further complicated by problems in the interpersonal realm blocking the progress of the task activity realm. For example, lack of tolerance and animosity amongst members influences the generating of creative solutions which in turn, influences the quality of the work being undertaken. What is clear is that the interpersonal and task realms are highly interrelated and interdependent, with progress in one affecting the other, thus ultimately impacting on the group's ability to move forward in the next stage.

While Tuckman presents his model within a rigid sequence of stages, it is possible under certain circumstances for different stages to be abbreviated and/or passed over. Review of the literature on groups, suggest that not all groups follow a full developmental sequence and that some who are "well acquainted with one another or with the task, seem to skip the orientation or forming stage" whereas others "accomplish very little productive work, missing the performing stage" (Cissna, 1984).

3.   How Groups Get Stuck

Tuckman in no way proposes successful methods for resolving each sequence. Nor does he suggest that stages reoccur, or that unresolved issues get recycled or reworked. He merely describes the behaviour of members in groups. He leaves it up to the reader to decide **how and why** a group gets stuck. One could therefore assume that a group could progress "unhealthily" from one stage to the next.

The following is an attempt on my part to identify some issues and concerns that could result in a group's getting stuck. While most of these issues have been linked to Tuckman's stages of group development, a few have not, as they represent concerns that could be experienced in any of the stages.

A.   When a group or leader neglects to deal with external causes of group anxiety e.g., budget cuts, threat of job loss, shift in task demands, eviction, illness or death of members etc., this may result in a group's getting stuck. As the unspoken issues begin to dominate, the group begins to regress. Signals of this occurring may be marked by absenteeism, recycling of old issues, resistance or apathy on the part of group members.

B.   In open-ended groups, where new members are regularly admitted, formation issues of dependence and orientation get recycled regularly. Unless a group has developed a structure to handle this, it can get stuck in the formation stage constantly providing for new members' dependence and orientation needs. On the other hand, if a group chooses to barrel along and ignore the needs of newcomers, it can get stuck further along the way, for under these conditions, new members do not become effective for a long time.

C.   Storming periods provide an arena for group members to work through issues of power, authority, and control-essential skills for the group's future. These issues get played out in differences of opinion as to task direction, and in the interpersonal conflicts that result from these sharp differences. Unless members are able to work through these conflicts, the group can get stuck or bogged down in this stage.

If the group chooses to abbreviate this stage, because it is too anxious to get the problem solved, or because members aren't willing to work through conflicts, these unresolved issues get recycled, resulting in the group getting stuck further along the way. This is evidenced in the norming stage where expression of opinions, sharing of perspectives and values emerge, or in the performing stage, where the group needs to work as a unit to achieve its goal.

D. Homogeneous groups (members who hold similar or comparable views, ideas, values and orientations) may have an easier time in the forming stage (search for commonalities) and the storming stage (expression of sharp differences), but a more difficult time in the norming stage (expression of opinions and perspective taking) and the performing stage (expression of creativity and challenge) where diversity of opinion is an asset. Unless the task facing the group requires uniformity, one can assume that homogeneous groups are more likely to get stuck at the norming and performing stages.

Conversely, heterogeneous groups (members who hold diversified or disparate views, ideas, values and orientations) may have a more difficult time and get stuck in the forming and storming stages, but a less difficult time in the norming and performing stages.

4.   Norms

What are norms? What role do they play in groups? What influence do they have on a group's development? What is important to know about them? How do they develop? What do they comprise of? These are just a few examples of questions that are often asked about norms. In the following paragraphs I shall try to define, describe and discuss some areas that need to be covered, in order to bring a more comprehensive understanding of Tuckman's third stage of group development, Norming.

Norms are agreed upon or shared beliefs by members of a group on such matters as: how to behave, value judgments about what should and should not be done, and how to maintain social relations (Shaw, 1981). Words commonly associated with norms are "ought, should, must, or better" (Shepherd, 1964). Some norms may be explicit, that is to say, ones that are publicly stated, out on the table and adhered to, whereas others are implicit in that no one acknowledges them, yet everyone adheres to them. Implicit norms are hardest to change, mainly because they are adhered to, yet not acknowledged. Tuckman (1991) subdivides norms into static and dynamic ones. Static ones represent norms that are unchanging, stable and firmly rooted, whereas the dynamic ones shift as needs, circumstances and conditions prescribe. (See Figure V-8 for further examples of the four types of norms.)

Explicit Norms - Norms that are considered explicit are ones that are agreed upon by virtually all members of a group. These are often referred to as "highly crystallized" norms. To come up with a comprehensive list is difficult, as each group's explicit norms are directly related to the type and focus of each group. For example, a Bible study group may have an explicit norm of starting with prayer, and a committee working on a task force may start with the previous session's minutes, whereas a Girl Guide group may start with a theme song. All are explicit norms, each peculiar to their own setting.

The following is an attempt to list some explicit norms that may cut across a range of contexts and hold under varied conditions of composition, size, duration, and focus. Some general examples touch areas such as: contracting basis of group, decision making, assignment of responsibilities, productivity expectations, dress code, choice of decision-making, guidelines for participation and discussion, methods of appraisal and assessment, criteria for joining group, hours of work and practice, ground rules (standards), structuring of a session, time and venues of group meetings, and evaluation of program, etc.

Implicit Norms - These norms are considered implicit only when they are frequently exhibited behaviours by most group members. Cartwright & Zander (1968) call them "mainstream" behaviours found acceptable to a group. Some examples of implicit norms found in groups are: in-joking, silence, "yessing," seating arrangements, methods of decision making, cooperation, competitiveness, complying with the group, teasing, loyalty, methods of resolving differences, submissiveness to authority, defying rules, openness to new ideas, enjoyment of food and refreshments, special privileges, ways of handling conflict, blaming, lateness, absenteeism, and turnover.

While Tuckman places the process of "norming" in a distinct stage, in reality norms are continuously in the process of evolving. Often the forming stage sets the pattern of what is acceptable and what is not. It is at this stage that the leader plays an important role in the modelling of healthy and constructive norms. It is also at this stage, that assumptions imported and shaped from previous experiences by group members begin to influence the development of norms. For example, if I believe groups are bad then those expectations will influence my contribution (or lack of) to the forming of the group. Norms will emerge that are defensive reactions to these expectations, and therefore, influence how the group will function.

The development of norms that get solidified in the norming stage is influenced by how the storming stage has been handled and resolved. If a group ignores signs of conflict and pockets of difficulty it is experiencing, or if it gets bogged down in the storming stage, the norms that emerge are often restrictive, i.e., everything, however small has to be checked out in the group for approval before a decision for action is made. If, however, the group has been able to resolve or recognize its conflicts, norms for handling conflict and maintenance begin to emerge, with members starting to realize what each can do for each other in service of the group's goal.

Norms do not always reflect member needs. In fact, in some groups it is not uncommon to have norms which conflict with the needs of its members. For example, in some task groups, the expression of feelings is discouraged, in others, the interaction amongst members is dissuaded. In certain groups, (Luft, 1984) one does not openly disagree with the leader, yet in others, group status is attained by successfully defying persons with power.

The place and influence of norms in groups cannot be underscored sufficiently. It is a crucial part of the process, for it sets the pattern for the next stages, ultimately working towards or against its goal. When a group is able to set norms that are appropriate to its needs and purposes, this has a direct bearing on its effectiveness and on the well functioning of its members.

Examples of Group Norms in a Course of Understanding Group Behaviour

	Explicit (Stated and adhered to)	**Implicit** (Assumed and adhered to)
	Norms Followed with Few Reminders	**Procedures and Routines**
Static (unchanging)	• Time and venue of group meeting • Choice of decision-making • Contracting • Establishing ground rules • Productivity expectations	• Seating arrangements (ie: generally in a circle) • Transfer in or feeling check before session starts • Coffee break halfway through a session • Planned activities related to the focus
	Norms in Need of Occasional Reinforcement	**Interpersonal Behaviour that Needs Leader Intervention**
Dynamic (shifting as needs arise)	• No interruptions • Encouragement of interaction with one another • Expression of individual opinions • Giving and receiving of feedback • Absenteeism and lateness discouraged	• Expressions of anger • 'Scape-goating' of a person • Ignoring members' contributions • Active abuse towards others • Distorted communication that is overlooked or ignored

FIGURE V-8

5.   Adjourning

This stage is different from the others in that it comes regardless of the group's successful or unsuccessful negotiation of the previous stage. Termination has to take place. In fact, it forces the group's sequence into adjournment, and has little to do with what has gone on before.

The quality and content of adjournment however, is greatly influenced by the previous stage, particularly on how successful the task accomplishment has been in the performing stage. In groups that get arrested or bogged down at the storming stage, the adjournment stage can take on a blaming atmosphere, with members unwilling to take on responsibility for what has transpired. This stage may also be welcomed with relief, as members beat a hasty retreat from an experience they would prefer to leave behind them.

What is clear, is that the experiences of previous stages set the pace for the next stage, and impacts on how termination eventually gets played out in the adjourning stage. Poor orientation contributes to the development of unresolved conflicts and fans the wind of resistance, hostility, and anxiety in the storming stage. Unless dealt with, it quite often results in non-productive norms in the norming stage, impedes successful task accomplishment in the performing stage, and it leads to difficult, if not poor, termination in the adjourning stage.

Failure to disengage effectively often leads to a hollow, unfinished feeling in the future. Unless members gain some clarity and insight into these negative experiences, these develop into a set of self-fulfilling mental expectations, which influence future formation in other groups.

6.   Limitations

A limitation in Tuckman's model is that his theory is more a description of common trends derived from reviewing the literature than an analysis of data based on systematic observations of groups.

His dependence on existing research as a source of data gathering is reflected in his initial abstraction of his four stages. Since existing research at that time did not focus on the importance of separation concerns as an issue in group development, Tuckman saw performing as the final stage of a group's evolution. It was only when his work was updated on more recent studies ten years later, (Tuckman & Jensen, 1977) that a fifth stage of adjournment was added.

The studies which Tuckman reviewed had their own limitations. They primarily reflected group therapy and human relations settings. They consisted of observations of a single group by the therapist and/or trainee, were based on accounts formulated after the fact, and they were highly anecdotal, reflecting clinical bias.

In addition, the over-representation of therapy and human relations groups, and the under- representation of laboratory and natural groups, make the results difficult to generalize. It has been found however that goallessness and planned ambiguity (Egan, 1970) characterize the former, while specific goals and structure characterize the latter. These differences are bound to reflect the preoccupation and behaviours of members.

While Tuckman suggested that his model needed further testing, few studies could be found that set out to test his hypothesis. However, despite all this, his model is considered one of the most popular models of group development by participants, partly because they find his description of stages catchy, colourful, and concrete, and partly because it does seem to capture the essence of their experiences.

PERSONAL NOTES ON TUCKMAN

REFERENCES

Abrahams, J. (1949). Group psychotherapy: Implication for direction and supervision of mentally ill patients. In T. Muller (Ed.). *Mental Health in Nursing.* Washington, D.C.: Catholic Universal Press.

Bales, R. F. (1950). *Interaction process analysis: A method for the study of small groups.* Cambridge, Mass.: Addison-Wesley.

Barron, M. E., & Krulee, G. K. (1948). Case study of basic skill training. *Journal of Social Issues, 4,* 10-30.

Berne, E. (1963). *The structure and dynamics of organizations and groups.* New York: Grove Press.

Bradford, L. P. (1964 a). Trainer-intervention: Case episodes. In L. P. Bradford, J. R. Gibb & K. D. Benne (Eds). *T-group theory and laboratory method.* New York: John Wiley and Sons, Inc.

Bradford, L. P. (1964 b). Membership and the learning process. In L. P. Bradford, J. R. Gibb & K. D. Benne (Eds). *T-group theory and laboratory method.* New York: Wiley and Sons, Inc.

Cartwright, D., & Zander, A. (Eds.). (1968). *Group dynamics research and theory.* New York: Harper and Row.

Cissna, K. N. (1984). Phases in group development: The negative evidence. *Small Group Behaviour, 15,* 28.

Clarkson, P. (1991). Group image and the stages of group development. *Transitional Analysis Journal, 21,* 36-50.

Corsini, R. J. (1957). Methods of group psychotherapy. New York: McGraw-Hill.

Egan, G. (1970). *Encounter: Group processes for interpersonal growth.* Belmont, CA.: Brooks/Cole.

Gladding, S. T. (1991). *Group work: A counselling speciality.* Toronto: Collier MacMillan.

Hare, A. P. (1982). *Creativity in small groups.* London: Sage Publications.

Hearn, G. (1957). A process of group development. *Autonomous Groups Bulletin, 13,* 1-7.

Kellerman, H. (Ed.). (1981). *Group cohesion: Theoretical and clinical perspectives.* New York: Guine and Stratton.

Kelman, S. (1980). Prayer and process. *Religious Education, 75,* 462-473.

Kormanski, C. (1988). Using group development theory in business and industry. *Journal for Specialists in Group Work, 13*, 30-41.

Luft, J. (1984). *Group processes.* Palo Alto, CA.: Mayfield.

Mann, J. (1953). Group therapy with adults. *American Journal of Orthopsychiatry, 23*, 332-337.

Maples, M. F. (1988). Group development: Extending Tuckman's theory. *Journal for Specialists in Group Work, 13*, 17-23.

Martin, E. A., & Hill, W. F. (1957). Towards a theory of group development: Six phases of therapy group development. *International Journal of Group Psychotherapy, 7*, 20-30.

Napier, R., & Gershanfeld, M. (1981). *Groups: Theory and experience.* Boston: Houghton Mifflin.

Parker, S. (1958). Leadership patterns in a psychiatric ward. *Human Relations, 11*, 287-301.

Powdermaker, F., & Frank, J. D. (1948). Group psychotherapy with neurotics. *American Journal of Psychiatry, 105,* 449-455.

Schroder, H. M., & Harvey, O. J. (1963). Conceptual organization and group structure. In O. J. Harvey (Ed.). *Motivation and Social Interaction.* New York: Ronald Press.

Shaw, M. E. (1981). Group dynamics: The psychology of small group behaviour. New York: McGraw Hill.

Tuckman, B. W. (1965). Developmental sequence in small groups. *Psychological Bulletin, 63,* (6), 384-399.

Tuckman, B. W., & Jensen, M. A. (1977). Stages of small group development revisited. *Group and Organization Studies, 2,* 419-427.

Tuckman, B. W. (1991). *Educational psychology: From theory to application.* Montreal: Harcourt, Brace & Jovanovich.

Weber, R. C. (1982). The group: A cycle from birth to death. *NTL Reading Book for Human Relations Training.* Arlington: N.T.L. Institute.

SECTION II

PROBING THE PHENOMENON OF GROUP DEVELOPMENT

Understanding groups is the result of a cumulative and progressive set of experiences. It demands the discipline to stop long enough to look and eventually see what is going on within the group itself..... it is a never-ending kaleidoscope, a puzzle with missing pieces those with patience and tenacity will eventually be rewarded with insight, understanding, and influence. Those up to the challenge will be able to diagnose, intervene, and ultimately, help change what is happening.

Rodney W. Napier
& Matti K. Gershenfeld (1999)

VI. BINDING TOGETHER A MULTITUDE OF FACTS

Whether or not you can observe a thing depends upon the theory you use.
It is the theory which decides what can be observed.

-Albert Einstein

SYNOPSIS OF FIVE GROUP THEORIES

The first section of this book describes five theories of small group development: **(1)** Bion's work and emotion theory of group development, **(2)** Gibb's TORI theory of trust formation, **(3)** Lacoursiere's life cycle of groups, **(4)** Schutz's three dimensional theory of interpersonal and group behaviour, and **(5)** Tuckman's developmental sequence in small groups. These theories were chosen for their clarity, practicality and transferability. They hold true under varied conditions of group composition, size, duration and focus. They also explain shifts in work level, explore how groups get blocked and outline the dynamics behind the inescapable influence of a group's emotional underworld. Each of the following brief descriptions is a synopsis of the five theories.

BION

Bion's theory focuses on two simultaneous operations within the group: the work level and the emotional theme. These two modes are so interrelated that one never occurs without the other. Thus, at any given point, the group's work level is accompanied by an undercurrent of emotional modes. Groups focus on three basic themes: dependence on the leader, fight-flight reactions to a threat to the group and pairing among members for emotional support. These modes (dependency, fight-flight and pairing) often interfere with the work level of the group. In a mature group, the emotional modes, while not necessarily resolved, are neither expressed nor focused on, but channeled and redirected in service of the work at hand (Rioch, 1970). Central to Bion's theory is his concept of valency, which he introduced to describe an individual's attraction to a particular emotional mode. According to him, valency is developed in the earliest group in our lives - the family. This orientation in turn influences feelings and behaviour toward authority figures and other group members in later life.

Key Concepts
• Dependence
• Boundaries
• Valency patterns
• Shifts in image of authority
• Work appears in some combination with an emotional mode

152

GIBB

The central core of Gibb's theory has to do with trust - "the pacemaker variable" in the growth of the group, with fear as the single most crippling force working against this trust. This theory suggests that "it is the process of trusting rather than the content of the trust that strengthens the relationships within the group" (Smith and Berg, 1987). Gibb's notion of contrapuntal need systems (growth needs versus defense needs) is very useful to explain paradoxical behaviour in groups. This personal, group and organizational development theory is based on four interdependent modal concerns (acceptance, data flow, goal formation and social control), which get recycled and reworked throughout the life of the system. Growth occurs concurrently on all four modal concerns with trust and acceptance the catalysts for the development of the other three. It is the reduction of these modal concerns which produces growth and movement within the group.

> **Key Concepts**
> - Primacy & paradox of trust
> - Modal concerns
> - Opposing contrapuntal need systems
> - Growth of group dependent on growth of individual
> - Recycling of phases

LACOURSIERE

Lacoursiere's five-stage progressive model of group development is practical, flexible and instrumental. Each stage includes task and socio-emotional behaviour. The stages are named according to their predominant theme: orientation, dissatisfaction, resolution, production, and termination. Lacoursiere's discussion of negative orientation and its ripple effect provides a significant contribution in the area of non-voluntary attendance in groups. Pivotal to this theory is the concept of disequilibrium where with the growth of a group begins with an experience of a dilemma or with disconfirming information which if worked through, can lead to productive and useful work. His theory alerts us to the fact that while termination signals the ending process for the group, it does not necessarily signify that the group has come to the end of its full potential development (Anderson, 1985).

> **Key Concepts**
> - Negative orientation
> - Morale
> - Disequilibrium
> - Closing the gap between expectations and reality
> - Termination does not mean the group has completed its life cycle

SCHUTZ

This theory assumes that groups, like individuals, have three basic interpersonal needs, namely: inclusion, control and openness. It posits that these needs influence group behaviour. While all three areas are always present in a group, they are not always of equal salience. The central issue in the group is the area which is emphasized and played out most intensively. Typically groups move from an initial concern for inclusion to a focus on control issues and finally to preoccupations with openness. As a group gets underway, these interpersonal need areas are addressed at a higher level and in a shorter span of time. The preceding concern must be a least partially resolved before the group can proceed to the next dimensions. Schutz introduces the interesting notion that as the group nears closure it reverses its sequence and retraces its passage from openness through control to inclusion.

Key Concepts
• Membership
• Expressed vs. Wanted needs
• Goblet issues
• Compatibility
• Reversal of sequences

TUCKMAN

This linear five-stage theory is regarded by some as a life cycle model in that it parallels that of the birth to death cycle. Each stage (forming, storming, norming, performing and adjourning) represents two realms of group behaviour: group structure, which has to do with the way members interact and relate to one another, and task activity, which has to do with the work that has to be accomplished. These two realms play an important role in the way each stage is resolved with progress in one influencing the progress of the other. Problems in the interpersonal realm block the progress in the realm of the task activity. Tuckman's is the only theory that identifies the emergence of norms as a central and specific stage in a group's development. These norms include ones that are static and firmly rooted and/or dynamic ones that shift as needs and conditions prescribe. This development of norms is important for it sets the pattern for the next two stages, ultimately influencing the group in working towards or against its goals.

Key Concepts
• Querying competence of leader
• Resistance to demands of the task
• Polarization of issues
• Groupthink
• Norming as a phase

Rythms and Cycles in Groups

Theorist	Type of Group Development	Theoretical Framework	Description
Wilfred Bion	Pendular Model	The activities in the group are analyzed in terms of level of work and emotional content. **The emotional modes are:** • Dependence • Fight-flight • Pairing	This is an analytic model that stresses the shifts in boundaries within the group. The leader is not an active force in moving the group but rather somewhat of a blank page upon which members project their feelings about authority. In this Tavistock approach to groups, shifts in emotional modes occur depending on situational dynamics. As the emotional mode shifts, so does the image of authority.
Jack Gibb	Modal Concerns Model	Trust is the basic component on which this theory is built. This framework has **four modal concerns:** • Acceptance • Data flow • Goal formation • Control	Modal concerns represent universal concerns basic to human growth needs. These modal concerns are "continually recurring themes or processes" within the group. Growth occurs concurrently on all four modal concerns. Increased resolution of these concerns produces growth and development within the group.
Roy Lacoursiere	Progressive Life Cycle Model	**Stages are:** • Orientation • Dissatisfaction • Resolution • Production • Termination	These stages occur in regular sequence. While they overlap and blend one into another, the central concerns are quite separate and distinct. Once a stage is passed, issues central to that stage can reappear with traces of earlier stages seen in later ones.

Rhythms and Cycles in Groups Cont'd

Theorist	Type of Group Development	Theoretical Framework	Description
William Schutz	Spiral Model	**Phases are:** • Inclusion • Control • Openness	While all three interpersonal needs are always present in the group, they are not always of equal importance. The spiral movement in the model illustrates how they get dealt with at a higher level and in a shorter span of time. As these interpersonal need areas get resolved by the group, the development of that particular need is moved further along. This helps the group deal with these various interpersonal need areas in a progressively more mature manner.
B.W. Tuckman	Progressive Linear Model	**Stages are:** • Forming • Storming • Norming • Performing • Adjourning	Stages appear in a specific, rigid, and fixed sequence without a set time-frame. In some circumstances some stages may be shortened and /or passed over. Each stage is seen as unique but not separate or disconnected from the next; unresolved concerns in one stage weigh heavily on the next.

FIGURE VI-1

Sequential-Stage Theories and Recurring-Phase Theories

These five theories of group development represent two different approaches as to how groups develop and change over time. "Recurring-phase" theories, i.e. Bion, Gibb and Schutz, specify the issues that dominate group interaction that recur again and again. "Sequential-stage" theories, i.e. Lacoursiere and Tuckman, specify the typical order of the stages of group development.

Comparisons Between Sequential-Stage Theories and Recuring-Phase Theories

Sequential- Stage Theories		Recurring-Phase Theories		
Lacoursiere: Concerns about shifts in morale and the gap between expectations and reality.	**Tuckman:** Concerns about the relationship between interpersonal and task realms and their influence on norms.	**Bion:** Concerns about authority and the distribution of power in the group.	**Gibb:** Central concern is trust of self and others.	**Schutz:** Concerns related to three basic interpersonal needs.
Orientation	Forming	Dependency Flight	Trust/ Acceptance	Inclusion
Dissatisfaction	Storming	Counter-dependency Fight	Data Flow Goal Formation	Control
Resolution	Norming	Pairing	Control	Openness
Producitvity	Performing			
Termination	Adjourning			Reversal of sequence: Control Inclusion

FIGURE VI-2

157

VII. DEVELOPMENTAL AREAS IN GROUPS

There is nothing so practical as a good theory.

-Kurt Lewin

This story captures what I hope the following section of this book will achieve - a heightened respect for groups, a deeper understanding of group process and an awareness that groups, like people, can learn and grow.

The young assistant professor, not yet used to the letters Ph.D. following his name, had been hired by the large, urban university to teach courses in the behavioral sciences. He arrived on campus both excited about sharing his new wisdom and terrified that he was ill-equipped to deal with his students.

Before classes began, one of his colleagues asked if he had ever taken a course in group dynamics. Nonchalantly, he told her that he had had several experiences, though in truth he had no idea what she was talking about. His colleague invited him to join her group dynamics class as a student to help orient him, and out of courtesy he accepted, wondering how much more there was to learn after nearly seven years of graduate school in Psychology.

The course was like nothing he had ever experienced. The group members sat around in a circle attempting to learn about group behaviour simply by becoming a group. There was no other agenda, no text on which to lean, no rules, no predetermined roles or goals. The instructor sat quietly, observing the students as they struggled to define their goal and determine whether they were succeeding or failing. The void filled with students' identity, influence, purpose, and control. Occasionally the professor made an observation on the group's process, but she kept her contributions to a minimum. The lack of structure resulted in an explosion of feelings.

The young man was amazed at what he saw. In the fertile ambiguity of this unstructured environment, every kind of behaviour he had ever studied began to surface; the group became a true laboratory of human behaviour. Three-hour meetings took place once a week for thirteen weeks, and at every one the group faced a new crisis as it came to grips with issues of identify, trust, frustration, and power.

What amazed him most of all was his colleague's behaviour. Each week, she calmly threw out one or two brilliant, pointed observations that propelled the group to new levels of understanding. He was both grateful for her wisdom and angered by his own inability to see and understand what seemed obvious to her. She seemed to see deeply not only into the present but also into future events, while he floundered along with everyone else, struggling with whatever was blocking the group's purpose at any given moment. Long after the course ended, he confided to her that at times he had seen her as a cross between a witch and a magician - serene, all powerful, and one who somehow knew what would happen in the group, perhaps in all groups, before it even occurred.

Taken from "Groups Theory and Experience"
by Napier, R.W. & Gershenfeld, M.K. (1999, p. 424)

This is a wonderful description of group process, a poignant illustration of someone who encountered an experience incongruent with his expectation. It is an excellent commentary of the fine work done by someone who knew and understood groups, group process and the nature of planned group development.

160

The Impact of the Early Phase on Group Development

A window of opportunity won't open itself.
-David Weinbaum

It is evident from the different descriptions of early phases in a group, that beginnings seriously impact tone, atmosphere and data flow. This dynamic cannot be underscored sufficiently: beginnings matter! They set the stage for the work that needs to be undertaken. The onset of a group is a period of hope, trepidation and dependence. It is a time of data gathering about self, others, the leader and the related content. Personal histories and previous group experiences flavour first perceptions. It is through this lens that members begin to listen, take stock, and take action. During this early stage although task roles are high, work level is low and maintenance roles practically non-existent.

We note that the early phase in **Bion's** theory is characterized by concerns about authority and the distribution of power in the group. Since the leader is not an active force for moving the group but rather somewhat of a blank page on which members project their feelings about authority, it is not unusual for "childlike dependency" and flight to emerge. The experience of having a leader who does not conform to what is expected or familiar to members, catapults them into a state of disequilibrium. This encounter with reality is important, for the group needs to experience its own helplessness before it can begin to appreciate and build on its own resources. During this early phase, maintenance roles displayed by group members are non-existent and those exhibited by the leader are often only minimally present or absent. This can be a very stressful phase for both members and leader alike.

Tip

> **The effective leader, according to this framework, is one who is willing to risk the accusation of failing to lead.**

161

Lacoursiere's early phase of orientation is characterized by positive and unrealistic expectations, high morale, and the heavy reliance on the group leader for guidance, content, and structure. This is a healthy dependence for it propels participants to ask for ground rules and gives rise to group norms. Roles related to defining the task, giving and seeking information and giving and seeking opinions are predominant. Unrealistic positive expectations and negative orientation are influencing factors in this stage. The "encounter with reality" is often unpleasant, leading to disequilibrium. However, this rude awakening, while difficult, is useful. Individuals who enter the group with a negative orientation (forced or required participation and/or negative feelings about groups) find this experience not only unpleasant but a very difficult one to work through. The tendency of the group during this period to not engage in maintenance functions contributes to making this phase particularly challenging. Involvement for such reluctant members becomes minimal and trying to get them to become resourceful, effective and committed members is a challenge.

Tip	**Stated unrealistic expectations need to be addressed as soon as possible, since the greater the gap between members' expectations and the reality of the situation, the greater the disappointment.**

For **Schutz** the central concern in this individually oriented stage is one of inclusion, membership and prominence. Uppermost in people's minds is the desire to connect, the wish to belong and the need to be accepted by the group. The level of perceived acceptance influences commitment and involvement. As members strive to present themselves as favourably as they can, their observation of others is flavoured by prejudice, predisposition and projection. Dimock (1993, p. 11) observes this about this early stage "…some participants find this "getting acquainted" process easiest if they jump into the activities or discussion, while others find that sitting back and watching works best for them. This creates a split between over-and under participators and often becomes an issue in the group as the big talkers try to pressure the quiet members into talking more. While the words are about appropriate participation in the group, the *music* is about what participants need to do to become accepted members in the group." In open-ended groups where membership is not fixed (e.g. patient groups in hospitals where members regularly leave with new ones frequently coming in) the group may get stuck and group members may find it hard to move past this inclusion stage.

Tip	**Trying to skip and/or ignore inclusion concerns in service of the task does not work as unresolved inclusion needs will surface again and again until resolved.**

Tuckman's first stage, forming, incorporates all the discomfort and awkwardness found in any new situation where "one's ego is involved in new relationships" (Napier & Gershenfeld, 1999). This initial period is one of caution, uncertainty, "hesitant participation" (Corsini, 1957), "tentative interaction" (Maples, 1988), and self-consciousness. Strong expressions of dependency on the leader, or other high status members, for direction and clarification of goals and procedures emerge. During this stage, interdisciplinary teams show high dependency on the role relationships developed outside of the group, and on the fixed hierarchy of responsibilities that accompany these roles. This dependency on role to determine power boundaries fosters the development of submission. Where participation is compulsory, forced or involuntary, this initial stage is one of testing and dependence. It is preceded by a pre-stage of "unshared behaviour" (Martin & Hill, 1957) characterized by resistance, silence and hostility.

Tip	When forming splinter or sub-teams to undertake specific tasks, cross fertilize or mix the membership to ensure diversity.

According to **Gibb,** fear is the natural state at the onset of group formation, with the first concern facing an individual whether to trust (growth needs) or mistrust (defense needs). The tension arises from not knowing whether to respond to the fear component or the trust component. This mixture of hope and trepidation provides the ingredients for an initial climate of doubt and hesitation. It is not unusual during this early stage for individuals to devise ways to cover up their fears and mistrust. Listening gets clouded with fear, fostering the distortion of perception and suspicion about the motives of others. Breaking out of the bonds of mistrust is not easy since it is "only through trusting that trust is built." In Gibb's model of growth and development, the influence of the individual's trust assumptions becomes critical. As the individual moves from reduction of fear and resolution of anxiety, formation of trust begins to take place. Gibb sees this growth as reciprocal: one contributes to one's growth, one contributes to the growth of others.

Tip	Encourage the development of maintenance roles for this helps narrow the gap between what is expressed and what is wanted.

SUMMARY

All five theories outlined above indicate that the early phase of group development is characterized by unrealistic expectations, anxiety, discomfort and cautiousness. Pre-set notions, low trust and biases dominate this stage. It also includes a large amount of interaction directed toward the leader, a lack of listening, a lack of support for others' agendas, superficial politeness, a low level of openness about one's personal needs or feelings, and a preference for using "we" instead of "I" (Jane Moosbruker, 1987).

The Role of Conflict and its Potential for Growth

We had the experience but missed the meaning.

-T.S. Elliot

When it comes to dealing with conflict we can run, sweep it away or grow from it. The choice is ours to make. "Conflict, though ever-present, is one of those things we seldom discuss; it is like a family secret that's kept in the closet. Yet it flavours almost everything that happens" (Napier & Gershenfeld, 1999, p. 391). Conflict is the stuff of life. *It is normal! It exists! It is inevitable!*

It is not the presence of conflict that causes disastrous and unfortunate things to happen, it is the harmful and ineffective management of it. The general assumption in our society is that conflicts are bad and should be avoided. It is also presumed that a good group is one in which there are no conflicts among members. Without conflict, groups can be set in their ways and lose their effectiveness because they do not re-examine their procedures and their relevance to the needs and goals of their own members.

While it is evident from the theories covered in this book that the conflict stage is the most difficult of all the phases in a group's development, it is also the *most critical*, since it provides opportunities for growth, learning and relearning. This is a powerful stage; one that is feared, dreaded and mistrusted. The conflict creates disequilibrium, disruption and disturbance in the system. It is the bane of group members' experience and group leaders find it compelling, exacting and unsparing. It can have a profound impact on both the individuals' and the group's development.

Lacoursiere, Schutz and Tuckman suggest that this period provides an arena for group members to work through issues of power, authority and control; essential skills for the group's future. These issues get played out in differences of opinion on task direction and in the interpersonal conflicts that result from these sharp differences. This phase is coloured by rivalry, competition, factions, redrawn alliances, polarized opinions, "brittle linkages" (Powdermaker & Frank, 1948), turmoil, in-fighting and power struggles. This is a sharp contrast to the earlier phase of enthusiasm, hope, trepidation, optimism, "hesitant participation" (Corsini,1957), polite discourse and self-consciousness.

Gibb's theory refers to facades, distorted and restricted data flow, the emergence of gossip, preoccupation with boundary setting, extremes in slow and rapid decision-making, protecting one's turf, and the misperception of "busy work" as creative and productive work. Bion's analytic model points to a struggle with authority, attempts to manipulate the leader to lead, playing down ideas or opinions made by the leader, and carefully studied forms of rejection of authority, or denial of outside influence. Working through the roles and relations with the authority figure becomes a central battleground.

164

Feelings generated during this "emotional upheaval" period are frustration, anxiety, anger, resentment, fear, inadequacy, powerlessness, shock, animosity, discontent, bewilderment, tension, vulnerability, end so on. Maintenance roles are non-existent, individual roles are high (blocking, digressing, out-of-field) and task roles narrow down mainly to giving opinions, and testing feasibility. Morale is low.

Each of the five theories highlight particular issues dominating this period. With Gibb, members with low level trust assumptions struggle between two contrapuntal need systems: growth needs vs. defense needs. The tension stems from not knowing whether to respond to the fear component or the trust component. Breaking out of the bonds of mistrust is paradoxical, for in order for trust to develop it must **depend on itself** to get started (Smith and Berg 1987).

Within Lacoursiere's framework it is the "encounter with reality" that brings into sharp focus discrepancies between expectations and experience. Members try to quell and screen themselves off from realities that disconfirm their expectations, or try to respond to the challenge for change, whilst at the same time attempting to hold on to their initial expectations. It is this struggle of forces pulling in opposite directions that characterizes much of the dilemma experienced during this disconfirming period.

With Schutz the central concern is that of competence. The pre-occupation is with self-determination, avoidance of humiliation and the fear of "being found out." In order to move forward the group has to feel it can influence its own destiny, which means becoming responsible for decisions that influence its own future direction. Members' preoccupation with power and influence dominates with questions of "how much do I influence?" and "how much do I want to be influenced?" overriding everything. Issues accompanying these concerns involve leadership, competition, amount of structure and method of decision making.

This picture looks dismal, bleak and dark. But is it as bleak as it really looks? Far from it. We need to experience our helplessness before we can wisely use our strengths, we need to "let go" before we can "take in," we need to own our disease of certainty before we can appreciate the nature of flexibility, we need to grasp the inseparable connection between work and emotion before we can respect its powerful influence, and we need to experience the constraints of fear before we can know the freedom that comes with the release of trust.

I have called this the "gain" through "pain" stage. This period provides an arena for group members to work through issues of power, authority and trust, the resolution of which paves the way for healthy development in the area of intimacy, affection and openness. No matter how clear the task or structure of the group, how reasonable the demands of the situation, or how appropriate the interventions of the leader, the emotional upheaval of this stage seems to be a necessary precursor to the solid and creative work in which the group eventually begins to engage. It is essential that you learn to live with it, learn to work with it and learn to make it work for you. It is worth it!

The Two Faces of Conflict

"Run, Sweep or Grow"

Growth When Learning and Openness Emerge Out of Conflict	Stagnation When Learning is Blocked and Resistance Emerges Out of Conflict
The emergence of learning and openness out of conflict promotes change and growth within the individual and group.	The stagnation, when resistance and the blocking of learning emerge out of conflict, hardens positions and the quality of decisions gets lowered.
It increases productivity and maximum use of resources.	It encourages poor use of resources and ineffective use of time.
It fosters commitment and motivation to the task at hand.	It nourishes apathy and grudging and compliance.
It builds the team and strengthens risk-taking.	It constrains trust, cultivates hidden agendas and restricts data-flow between members.
It paves the way for the emergence of task and maintenance functions.	It optimizes preoccupation with boundary setting and protecting of one's turf.

FIGURE VII-1

166

The Power of the Work Phase

No member of a crew is praised for the rugged individuality of their own rowing.

-Ralph Waldo Emerson

What does "work phase" really mean? What does it stand for? What happens if a group does not reach this stage in its development? Has it failed its purpose? Has it neglected to fulfill its mandate? These important questions are often asked and need to be clarified. This stage has been mistakenly taken to mean that until a group has reached the work phase of its development, it does not begin its work of performing its task. In other words, the task that the group needs to accomplish is at a "stand still" until its members enter the work stage of the group's development.

This is a mistaken view albeit natural. Work is always going on in the group, be it Tuckman's initial formation stage, Schutz's control phase, Lacoursiere's resolution stage Gibb's modal concern of trust and acceptance, or Bion's emotional level of fight/flight. However, there is one crucial difference. The work is at a different level with productivity accompanied by positive feelings where the resources and skills of the group are used in a healthy balanced way.

Many of us have been in groups or teams in which our resources have never been used, recognized or appreciated, where our interventions have been ignored, where our contributions have been taken for granted and/or disregarded and where our presence has made little to no difference. Many of us have experienced the pain of being snubbed, looked right past and given no eye contact while others have been pointedly addressed even though we have been just as present. Many of us have been in situations where we have been isolated, brushed aside, overlooked in favour of someone less suited for a particular task or have been given responsibility yet have had our decisions overridden. Many of us have experienced the feeling of disengagement, grudging compliance and apathy over decisions compromised to the point that they are irrelevant. The list is interminable, the experiences indelible and the learnings invaluable. In such situations it is hard to give our best to the task, to search for excellence despite the experience, to remain focused and to maintain enthusiasm for the work at hand.

The above transactions do not transpire wittingly or regularly in a group that is fully engaged in the work phase of its development. This is not to say that such issues do not surface or that the group does not experience "recurring frustrations." They do; however, these frustrations are sporadic in frequency, with the group recognizing the dynamics more quickly. This awareness often spurs the group on to higher levels of functioning as feedback, insights and learning are translated into action.

So what does work phase mean? Lacoursiere suggests that this is the most productive stage in the group's life cycle. Time is used efficiently, ideas flow and are exchanged freely and easily, interaction is high, morale rises, playfulness is in evidence despite the seriousness which descends upon the group. Competition takes on a new meaning as members healthily engage in it but this does not get in the way of cooperation.

Schutz refers to this stage as openness where opinions are communicated in a direct and honest way and where opposing opinions are sought after. This new level of trust and openness releases the group's creative functional resources and unique abilities, paving the way for productive problem-solving. There is willingness to be influenced by others and a readiness to influence others. Members increasingly volunteer to take on tasks; working towards a group goal is seen as a corporate responsibility. Proposed solutions are tested and consensual validation is used.

For Tuckman, the general atmosphere during this "performing" period is one of support, openness and flexibility. The work structure of the group permits the creative "use of differences" (Hearn, 1957) with members freely expressing themselves without "censoring" their responses. Norms developed for handling conflict and maintenance emerge. Interdependence among members permits an interplay and flexibility in the roles taken.

Using Gibb's framework we note the influence of high trust, where diversity is appreciated as a potential strength and where tolerance of deviations is present. During this growth period members show vulnerability, conflict is openly acknowledged with the power structure becoming relatively open. Work is purposeful and problem-solving arises spontaneously in response to needs. In short, there is marked increase in member involvement and interdependence in role distribution and action planning.

Bion's increase in work level is captured by Dimock (1987) in this way, "The mature phase is one of integration, group flexibility, open expression of individual feelings, and task accomplishment" (p.75). The preoccupation with authority issues gives way to protective pairing, i.e., aligning oneself with those who have similar views and/or searching for commonalities between self and others. The collective tension, previously directed towards the authority figure, translates into cohesive energy and interdependence and the full use of the rich resources in the group.

During this work period there is high visibility of task functions and mutual task interaction resulting in role flexibility and a wide range of role distribution, further enhancing the group's capacity to engage in situational leadership. Depending on the type of group, i.e., therapy groups, human relation groups, learning or training groups, short-term problem-solving groups, task, work groups or committees, the group becomes a finely tuned instrument, directed to relevant task-related activities engaging in "realistic appraisal of what could be accomplished" (Tuckman & Jensen, 1977). Emphasis on evaluation of the group's product (Bales, 1950), assessment and testing of actions and proposals is directly linked to type and focus of group.

The productivity in this phase has to do with the flow and building together of various categories of need levels within the group. These fundamental need areas represent three levels: "team needs" (the building and maintaining of the team), "individual needs" (personal needs that are important to meet at the appropriate level) and "task needs" (getting the job done), (Adair, 1988).

In a team, members try and find or are forced to strike a balance between the three sets of needs. Most often, the balance is an uneasy and ever-changing one, creating tensions at the center of certain activities. When these three need levels begin to mutually feed on and replenish each other, the depth of work within the group deepens and the involvement and commitment of members strengthen while productivity and efficiency continue to rise.

Being part of such high energy, commitment and creativity is seductive, meaningful and rich. This is often experienced as a very powerful stage. The possibilities of "cutting edge" work undertaken in such a vibrant atmosphere are manifold. For this working system (the group) has now become a learning organization, invincible yet vulnerable, flexible yet cautious, realistic yet venturesome.

ADAIR'S THREE CIRCLES MODEL

The Inter-locking Nature of the Circles in the Diagram Below Emphasize Interdependence of the Three Need Areas

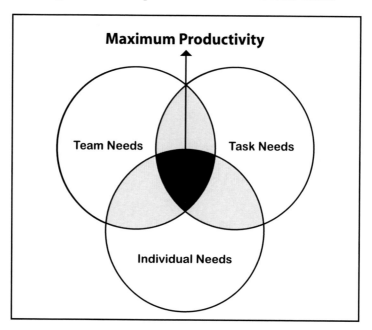

FIGURE VII-2

The above diagram illustrates the relationship and tension that often exists between team needs, individual needs, and task needs. The three domains can interact (see shaded area) and also remain separate. The fact that the area of complete convergence of needs is often small (the darkest area) is one reason why a group's rationality is such a rare phenomenon.

KEY FEATURES OF THE WORK PHASE

- Focused work with clarity of purpose and direction.

- Full use of members' resources.

- Marked increased in members' involvement and interdependence.

- Competition does not get into the way of cooperation.

- Balance between team needs, individual needs, and task needs.

FIGURE VII-3

What Does Resolution Really Mean?

We don't receive wisdom; we must discover it for ourselves after
  a journey that no one can take for us or spare us from.

-Marcel Proust

Lacoursiere's Life Cycle of Groups Theory is the only theory that specifically identifies a stage in the group's development as "Resolution". The fact that the other theorists did not include this in their framework raises interesting questions. Can we conclude that Bion, Gibb, Schutz and Tuckman did not observe this dynamic in their research on groups? Could they have perchance overlooked this developmental dimension?

On the contrary, while this might seem so on the surface, closer exploration of their data suggests that the building blocks that lead to this stage and the essence represented within it are all present within their theories. What are these building blocks? What is the essence represented in the resolution stage? What role does resolution play in propelling the group forward and onward? How does this dynamic appear in the other theories?

170

What we do know is that all five theories suggest that growth follows a period of crisis and that this in turn influences the work of the group. Lacoursiere calls this crisis "encounters with the limitations of the experience," Tuckman refers to it as "resistance to the task and the leader," Schutz identifies it as a "period of preoccupation with control, competency and power," Bion "self-preserving negative cycle of low trust."

Essentially, "resolution" within the context of these theories represents a turning point that influences the group's functioning. It is not so much an event that occurs but a cumulative set of experiences that finally drives home a truth, a reality, a message which had been present all along but incapable of being seen. The impact that follows is powerful. The resulting paradigm influences tone, flow of events, actions and decisions. It brings direction and purpose to the group, which in turn act as a catalyst propelling the group to enter a deeper, wiser and more meaningful way of working and fulfilling its mandate.

Reconciling the gap between reality and experience constitutes the fabric of our lives. When we fail to rise to the occasion, when we turn a blind eye to what we see, when we turn a deaf ear to what we hear, when we choose not to entrust ourselves to others, we stunt our growth, limit our potential and become less than what we really are.

Concomitantly, when we allow ourselves to own the realities of the situation and permit ourselves to "let go," we enter a zone of new and renewed ways of perceiving and experiencing life. Our lenses change, our boundaries shift and a new set of rules permeates our system. Groups go through similar cycles and processes leading to growth and development; like individuals, they are affected by a wide range of forces at any given time.

The processes involving resolution that serve to start an unfolding process of learning are present in all five theories previously discussed. I have identified eight processes and/or turning points that appear in these theories. These are: **(1)** owning, **(2)** letting go, **(3)** shifting of paradigm, **(4)** norm setting, **(5)** structure development, **(6)** consensual decision-making, **(7)** acceptance of diversity, and **(8)** commitment. These areas are processed throughout the life of the group and continually flow and build on each other. What is important to note is that processes of "owning" and "letting go" compose the catalyst for the development of the other six areas.

Dimensions Involved in the Resolution Stage

1. Owning	Acceptance of gap between initial expectations and actual team reality.
2. Letting Go	Willingness and readiness to let go of expectations that do not fit the situation.
3. Shifting of Paradigm	Shift in perception of need, followed by attitude change and openness.
4. Norm Setting	Norms for handling conflict and maintenance begin to emerge.
5. Structure Development	Structure and procedures are sorted through and collectively decided on.
6. Consensual Decision-Making	Movement towards consensual decision-making.
7. Acceptance of Diversity	Acceptance of others and growing respect for individual differences.
8. Commitment	Grudging compliance and/or resistance shift to genuine commitment.

FIGURE VII-4

The Hidden Dimensions of Endings

We shall not cease from exploration and the end of all our exploring
will be to arrive where we started and know the place for the first time.

-T.S. Eliot

Probably the most important and complex stage of a group's development is termination. Considering the limited research done in this area one would hardly imagine that this is so. While the other theories refer to this stage, Lacoursiere's theory is the only one that pays significant attention to it. Tuckman (1965), in his original work, developed and identified four stages ending with performing. It was Jensen (Tuckman and Jensen, 1977) who recognized the omission of a fifth stage, appropriately named adjournment, which Tuckman added to his original phases.

Why is this stage so important? Why has so little been done by way of research in this area? Napier and Gershenfeld (1999) observe that termination is a difficult stage to study as most groups which were researched were "temporary one-time laboratory groups without an organizational context." While this is true, it is rather strange that so much attention has been placed on the development and maintenance of groups but not on their endings.

Lacoursiere draws attention to the fact that while termination may signal the end of the group's experience it does not necessarily mean that the group has completed its task. When the task is not completed the outcomes are usually negative, particularly if the group is still in the dissatisfaction stage or in the midst of the production stage. Morale fluctuates depending on task completion.

Tuckman and Jensen (1977) discuss modes of disengaging from the team. Depending on the type and focus of the group, termination takes the form of "tying up loose ends" or "divestment of emotional energy" from the rich experience of group cohesion (Clarkson, 1999). Where there has been little to no investment in task completion, the disengagement is void of achievement and termination is viewed with "relief and liberation."

Gibb's and Bion's open ended theories do not specifically deal with termination but refer to the group's growth, maturity and increased work level with time, whereas Schutz notes the recycling of interpersonal needs and the reversal in sequence as the group retraces its passage from openness through control to inclusion (O-C-I).

In the university department where I teach, most of our courses are framed within a group development context. Within the department, groups are used for different reasons in different courses. In some courses they are used as a vehicle for learning a particular subject interactively. In courses that are specifically designed to study groups, they are set up not only as a vehicle for learning but also as a context to learn about group functioning and in most cases, as a forum to develop observational skills to facilitate understanding of their particular group. Obviously, these are powerful contexts to learn from, often giving learners useful tools to apply in their outside world. These one-time groups set up to learn about group functioning are usually given an opportunity to bring meaning to the closure of their work together as a team.

In general, with most one-time groups, the end stage signifies closure to the task and a shift in the relationships. This is a period of reflection, sharing of learnings and insights, and in some cases doubts, reservations and intentions. As in most of the stages, the process in the termination stage varies according to the focus of the group. However, in all these groups, termination involves coming to terms with both its accomplishments and limitations in relation to the task. This means a period of assessment and realistic appraisal of what has been done and what yet needs to be done. Despite the fact that these are one-time groups, all individuals "move back into a larger organizational context to work with similar and different co-workers." This dynamic can never be under-estimated for what has transpired in their one-time group experience, the way the work was accomplished, how the relationships were handled, and whether the closure reflections brought insight, influences powerfully members' future work in teams.

My experience as a facilitator/leader/consultant in one-time groups has shown me that unless I have made it part of the actual agenda, the group does not initiate this termination process nor understand its significance until they experience it. What happens with disturbing regularity is apologies discreetly whispered to me of prior arrangements to leave early. These announcements are usually peppered with comments such as "I have to leave earlier but will be here for the most important part" or "please understand it is not that I don't want to be here, but I need to leave before the end" or "that was the only time I could have made that appointment, I am so sorry" or "in any case I can't be missing much." I am coming to the conclusion that "closure" is a difficult dynamic of life and that most of us have "unfinished business" with endings, transitions and letting go. Ironically research has only left this as "unfinished business."

As for groups linked to a larger organizational context, closure occurs in many different ways. Committees often complete their task of assessing their product but not their process. This is a sad commentary for these very same people move on to other groupings with similar and different colleagues to fulfill new mandates, thus contributing to the functioning of a department or a unit. Obviously private insights do take place and get transferred, but what is missing is the collective reflection that raises the quality of the system into a learning organization. Other types of endings continually occur as colleagues retire, are assigned elsewhere, move on to other interests, work units are reorganized, etc. "At each ending point groups have the opportunity (rarely taken) to evaluate and reflect on the work or relationships. They have a chance to share feelings and thoughts, give feedback, celebrate effort and achievement, and reflect on learnings" (Napier and Gershenfeld 1999, p. 443).

Termination, whether in temporary one-time laboratory groups or groups linked to a larger organizational context, plays an important role in the on-going underpinnings of a system both on an individual and/or organizational basis. Not to build-in this process is to miss the opportunity of maximizing quality, involvement and task effectiveness. Dealing with the assessment of the product yet neglecting a reflection on the process, only serves to entrench the group and its members in its set ways of functioning. When this happens work teams eventually lose their effectiveness because they do not re-examine their procedures and their relevance to the needs and goals of their own members.

VIII. THE NATURE OF GROUP DYNAMICS

The greatest problem of communication is the
illusion that it has been accomplished.

-George Bernard Shaw

The Relationship Between Work and Emotion

Two roads diverged in a wood and I took the one less traveled by,
and that has made all the difference.

-Robert Frost

All five theories stress the importance and link between work and emotion. **Bion's** framework refers to two simultaneous operations within the group: the work level and the emotional level. These two modes are so interrelated that one never occurs without the other. The emotional quality often determines the work level and vice versa. Dimock (1987, p.73) describes this interplay between these two levels in this way: "A group where members are concerned about their status and are directing fight to that concern, probably produces little work. Likewise, a group with an overwhelming task might handle it with emotional flight." In another example Dimock suggests that while a group may not be openly verbalizing the emotional theme of flight, the way it chooses to go about accomplishing its task may indicate the contrary.

In **Lacoursiere's** framework each of the five stages includes task and socio-emotional behaviours. The task behaviours are related to structure and procedures put in place to accomplish the work at hand whereas the socio-emotional behaviours are related to reactions and interactions of group members toward the task, the group leader and/or other members. For example, a group entering the resolution stage may decide to use Robert Rules of Order to monitor flow of interaction and discussions. For some, this decision comes as a relief for it ushers in more structured communication, efficient use of time and less likelihood of members digressing from issues at hand. For others, this shift in procedure may be perceived as a regressive stance robbing the group of synergistic dialogue and a more natural flow of discussions.

Similarly, **Tuckman's** five stages of group development include two realms of group behaviour. One is related to that of interpersonal relationships (group structure) and the other to the work (task activity) of the group. These two realms play a substantial role in the way each stage is resolved, with progress in one influencing the progress of the other. Thus in the forming stage a group moves through testing and dependency (problems inherent in developing relationships among members) as well as managing information and functions critical to the task (issues related to the work that has to be accomplished).

As can be seen it is difficult to consider the development of a group without stressing the interdependence of work and emotion within a group. These two simultaneous operations co-exist and interrelate throughout the life of the group.

The Recycling and Reappearance of Themes

The real voyage in discovery consists not
in seeking new landscapes, but in having new eyes.

-Marcel Proust

Do groups neatly cycle through phases of group development? The answer is no! Are the phases predictable and easy to identify? The answer is yes! Do groups go through several phases and then repeat the cycle again and again throughout their history? The answer is sometimes.

The group theories dealt with in this book are either sequential-stage theories or recurring- phase ones. These processes are not contradictory but simply indicate the type of growth movement in the group. Basic predictable life themes are reflected in these stages and since issues underlying these themes never get completely resolved, they periodically reappear depending on the dynamic encountered by the group. If we assume that groups like people grow, get stuck, regress, deny, resist, pretend, rush through or are ready to face psychosocial crises and/or basic needs related to a group's functioning, then the reappearance of themes is not an unusual phenomenon.

While Bion does not imply any particular sequence to the order of the emotional modes appearing in his framework, his schema does contain discernible phases and typical sequences that a group goes through, e.g., dependency, fight-flight and pairing in response to perception of authority figures. These emotional modes shift and reoccur, varying in duration. As the emotional mode changes, so does the image of authority. In a mature group the level of work increases as the emotional modes "get used in the service of work task" (Rioch, 1970), whereas in a less mature group deriving particular satisfaction from an emotional mode can get stuck and/or may even remain stuck. An important characteristic in Bion's framework of groups is that the emotional mode refers to the entire group and not the individual. While this may be reflected in a member's behaviour, the individual is merely "acting out" what exists in the group (Durkin, 1964).

Schutz's framework assumes that groups have three basic interpersonal need areas of inclusion, control and openness and that they appear in that order. The sequence is a temporal one. Each dimension requires that the previous one be in operation before it can be worked on, and at least partially resolved before it can proceed to the next one. As the group gets underway, these need areas get dealt with at a greater depth and in a shorter span of time. However, while all three areas are always present in a group, they are not always of equal salience. Thus, over time, needs recede in the background and what gets played out and emphasized is the central issue in the group. Here we note how an individual's unresolved need area can make it impossible for the group to proceed further, thus influencing a group's preoccupation with a particular phase. This is most evident in the control phase where power struggles begin to emerge.

179

Lacoursiere's developmental stage theory is a progressive life cycle model of group development. His five stages occur in a regular sequence and while they overlap and blend one into another, they are quite distinct and separate. Nonetheless, this does not mean that once a stage is passed, that issues central to that stage do not reappear. They often do with traces of earlier stages seen in later ones and vice versa. When the group is of shorter duration, open-ended or the task impersonal and concrete, the sequence becomes blurred. This is particularly true with respect to the resolution and termination stages which get "masked or distorted" (Hill & Gruner, 1973) or even omitted. Lacoursiere draws attention to how an individual's cycle can differ and influence the life and growth of a group particularly if several members simultaneously go through the same cycle.

Tuckman's five stage model is a progressive linear one. Stages appear in a specific order, are unique, but not separate or disconnected from the next. Unresolved concerns in one stage weigh heavily in the next, influencing the group's ability to move on constructively. The interpersonal and task realms are highly interrelated and interdependent with progress in one affecting the other, thus ultimately impacting the group's ability to move forward to the next stage. Tuckman presents his model within a rigid sequence of stages. He does not suggest that stages reoccur, or that unresolved issues get recycled or reworked. He merely describes the behaviour of members in various stages.

Gibb's theory is not a stage theory but a growth directed humanistic one representing four modal concerns. Growth occurs concurrently on all four dimensions, with optimal growth occuring when "deepest and earliest" modal concerns arise in the following order: acceptance, data flow, goal formation and social control. Gibb's theory of trust formation focuses on self-acceptance as one of the most crucial factors in the development of the group. His theory is based on the central assumption that we cannot trust others unless we trust and accept ourselves first. Thus, the influence of the individual's trust orientation is key to the group's growth. Growth is a directional movement - one contributes to one's own growth and the growth of others. Reciprocity is key. However, to be truly effective, growth has to occur for all individuals involved in the group.

A common pattern between the theories is the inescapable connection between phases, stages and modal concerns. These developmental orientations potentially propel or retard the growth and maturity of the group. How these themes are dealt with nourishes or diminishes the quality and depth of the ensuing theme.

An outstanding difference between the theories is the central role an individual member plays in the development of the group.

IX. THE SATURATED SELF

The last human freedom is to choose one's
attitude in any given set of circumstances.

-Victor Frankl

The "I Hate Groups" Phenomenon

We first shape our buildings and then they shape us.

-Winston Churchill

Group hate is real. I am constantly meeting people who openly declare their aversion for groups and their antipathy towards working in groups, teams and/or meetings. To them working in a group is frustrating, unproductive and a "necessary evil." This attitude prevails whether they are part of a team on a voluntary or involuntary basis, whether they are a member or in a position of leadership within the team. Why is this so? What makes people dread meetings and find them of "marginal value" or "not worth the time?" (Mosvick & Nelson, 1987). What makes students distrust and dislike working in groups, even fearing groups? I often ask myself this question, particularly as I teach in a university department well known for its group work, with most of our courses framed within a group development context.

Here are some issues that contribute to the **"I hate groups"** syndrome:

- wasting considerable time having too many meetings,
- striving for consensus over obvious issues,
- making compromises which no one is pleased with,
- listening to discussions that have become a series of monologues,
- dealing with conflict by making it personal,
- experiencing cynical attitudes that disrupt team relationships,
- showing little sensitivity for the need for balanced interaction,
- watching under-motivated members squeeze by without contributing their share,
- digressing from the issues at hand,
- setting unrealistic goals,
- working alone and accomplishing more than a team in a much shorter time,
- sweeping conflict under the rug,
- focusing on the person not the problem,
- coming back to dead issues,
- ostracizing a member to induce conformity,
- suppressing and avoiding disagreements,
- promoting rigid conformity and de-emphasizing individuality,
- ignoring or suppressing feelings that emerge out of work together,
- resenting a member who is much more productive than others,
- **ending a group or team experience in the dissatisfaction/control stage.**

And this is only a partial list! Are groups as inept as this acerbic assessment indicates? Are groups assembled together to stymie progress and serve as roadblocks to effective problem solving? Absolutely not! What do we know about teams? We know groups and teams are here to stay. We know that groups have always been the building blocks of organizations with team projects becoming the principal method of managing work. We know that the paradigm of teaching is changing from lecture and individual work to cooperative learning (Johnson, Johnson, & Holubec, 1998a, 1998b), with students of all ages being asked to work in small groups to maximize both their own learning and the learning of others. We also know that teams typically achieve higher quality results than individuals working alone.

Given that this book deals with theories of small group development, I want to focus on my last point listed on the "I hate groups" syndrome that is, "ending a group or team experience in the dissatisfaction/control stage." I am doing so deliberately as I have noted with some dismay that a good number of our students terminate their group experience in the dissatisfaction stage. This can be very devastating. This experience feeds into the "larger organizational memory for better or for worse" (Napier & Gershenfeld, 1999). In this case, for worse weakens members' ability and desire to work in a group setting in the future. Often this signals the beginning of their engagement in the negative orientation. This cycle is hard to break unless there is some reflection and understanding by the individual of what took place, leading to learning that can be applied to future work in groups.

Sorenson (1981) suggests that group hate diminishes among members who receive training about working in groups. This means understanding group process, becoming sensitive to group phases, knowing group dynamics theory and developing small group skills. Realistic expectations get developed which in turn help to minimize the obstacles and capitalize on the strengths in the group. This means being able to diagnose, intervene and ultimately, help change what is happening. When it comes to group functioning, knowledge gives power.

The Best Potential in "ME" is "WE"

The strength of the wolf is in the pack.
-Rudyard Kipling

Someone once said that the ratio of "We's" to "I's" is the best indicator of the development of a team. Is this really so? Does this mean that our personal needs within a group ought to be in service of the team? Does this mean that the collective is more important than the individual? Does this mean that my best interests are served when I take a back seat to what I would like to see happening? Does this mean I don't count? Does this mean that others within the team come before "me"? Where does the "I" fit in the "we"? Where does my uniqueness play a role? How can I contribute if I cannot be myself? What does the balance of needs mean if the scales tip away from me? How can I keep my integrity when my values are violated, when what I stand for does not count, when what I believe in is made light of? Where am I in this equation? How can I best serve my team's needs when my needs are being suppressed? How can I serve the task needs within the team when my views, resources and skills are not being used? Last, but by no means least, how do I differentiate between what I need to "let go of" in service of the team and what I need "to hold onto" in service of the team?

183

These are thoughts many of us have entertained at some point, but rarely voiced. Underlying these reflections are deep feelings we dare not express, that we dare not contemplate. We have walked with them, made friends with them and lived with them. They have influenced our actions, our reactions and our attitudes. They have sometimes even compromised our search for excellence, the quality of our contributions and the genuineness of our commitment.

So what does the "**best potential in *me* is really *we*"** actually mean? I have frequently pondered this question. My work in groups as a professor whose specialty is group dynamics has given me much food for thought. Coupled with my applied approach to teaching, untold opportunities to observe, listen and reflect have been laid at my door. As a consultant I have seen, worked with, and worked on this issue countless times. Lastly, my involvement as a colleague in departmental committees, either as a member or a chair, continues to remain my best teacher. My observations and experiences have taught me important lessons. I am still learning them. Here are some of them.

Being a member in a team means being in a collective - a collective that has a purpose and a goal. Whether we are part of the team on a voluntary or involuntary basis is a moot point, important as this may be. Our very membership suggests responsibility and involvement. Being a member suggests presence, listening and perspective taking. It means stepping out of ourselves in order to be in touch with ourselves, in order to be in touch with the issues at hand in the team and in order to be in touch with the underlying interpersonal currents ever present in the team. It means switching the station and pressing the "inside-out" button of our remote control in order to access the "outside-in" one. Being a team member means taking ourselves, our role, our assigned task, and our team colleagues, seriously.

The few times I have been able to enter into the essence of all of the above has brought out the best in me. My concern in such situations has strangely been more for the others than for myself and has felt good. Those have been the times when I have put more energy into trying to understand than being understood. Those indeed were the times when the best potential in "Me" became really "We." Those were the times when I felt most vulnerable yet strong. Those were the times I dared to entrust myself to others and by so doing found my voice.

I found words to speak my piece, to make my own needs known and was in touch with what I needed to "let go of" in service of the team and what I needed "to hold onto" in service of the team. I glimpsed, I understood, I took action.

Groupthink - The Illusion of Agreement

The important thing is to not stop questioning.

-Albert Einstein

The French scientist Jean-Henri Fabre's experiment with caterpillars (Van Ekeren, 1988) is an excellent illustration of groupthink behaviour - a self-limiting, self-imposed group phenomenon that some groups suffer, often unbeknownst to them (Beebe and Masterson, 2003). Groupthink results in ineffective consensus and poor decisions made in the interest of group solidarity with the consequence that the group "loses its own powers of critical analysis," (Dubrin, 2001), thus perpetuating the illusion of agreement. History is replete with examples of decisions which led to major disasters and where various decision-making bodies became trapped in their "dynamics of groupthink:" (Nixon and Watergate, Kennedy and the Bay of Pigs, Roosevelt and Pearl Harbour, Johnson and the Vietnam War, and Churchill and the invasion of Dunkirk).

The term groupthink was coined by sociologist Irving Janis (1971, 1972, 1982). Essentially it represents "the collective striving for unanimity that overrides group members' motivation to realistically appraise alternative courses of action." Conflict avoidance, concurrence-seeking by group members and the insulation of the group from outside influences or the pressure of outside circumstances and persons are common critical factors contributing to the groupthink process.

While research does not convincingly support the theory of groupthink, I have observed this phenomenon in our student groups regularly. In many group courses students plan, design and give leadership to a group presentation. Periodically, the essence of the presentation totally misses the point. It is as if group members dismissed data they did not want to hear and became blinded to what needed to get done. Feedback is usually met with disbelief and incredulity. They were sure they had been on the right path, had used consensus to ensure commitment, and no one had disagreed. In fact these groups have often considered themselves a highly cohesive team, taking pride in being open with each other and getting along well with each other. Their meetings were usually smooth, they understood each other, decisions were made easily and they had been supportive and encouraging of members' ideas and proposals. On closer questioning it becomes obvious that while the group had reached consensus it did not necessarily mean that **all** the members **truly** agreed. The list is endless, the experiences vary but the message and the patterns remain the same. Dubrin (2001) aptly describes this crippling dynamic this way:

> Groupthink is an extreme form of consensus. The group atmosphere
> values getting along more than getting things done. The group thinks as
> a unit, believes it is impervious to outside criticism, and begins to have
> illusions about its invincibility (p.124).

Within an on-going team the effects of 'apparent' consensus are cumulative until the norm of the team becomes 'groupthink'; individual resources become weaker and decisions less effective.

Dr. Fabre's story is worth repeating for it vividly drives home the issues of groupthink and alerts us to the pitfalls we can so easily fall into when it comes to this phenomenon.

There was once a French scientist, named Jean-Henri Fabre who had a very interesting passion in life; he studied caterpillars. At one point in his research, Dr. Fabre conducted an experiment that involved processionary caterpillars - wormlike creatures that travel in long, unwavering lines, at the same pace and cadence.

One day, Dr. Fabre placed a group of these wormy creatures onto the thin rim of a large flowerpot, forming a circle of caterpillars. In other words, the leader of the group of caterpillars was nose to tail with the last caterpillar in the slow, non- ending procession. The scientist found it difficult to figure out which was the leader and which were the followers.

During this entire day, Dr. Fabre watched the caterpillars go around and around in a circle without ever stopping. Later that night, he went home. The next morning when he arrived at his laboratory he noticed that the caterpillars were still going around in a circle.

Then, Dr. Fabre placed a supply of food in the centre of the flower pot. Even this did not detour the caterpillars. Day after day, night after night, the caterpillars paraded around and around. Seven days later they finally stopped. Do you know why? Because they started dying; they died of starvation.

Excerpt taken from "The Speaker's Source book,"
by G. Van Ekeren (1988)

The lessons in this story are many. And as with many lessons of life they are simple yet complex. The caterpillars blindly kept following the one ahead of them. They worked hard - very hard. They never gave up yet they were tired. They never stopped but kept up their pace and their place. They were hungry but did not see the food that was near by and available for their eating. The caterpillars never looked up nor around.

How often have we blindly followed our team members without putting serious thought into what is being proposed? How often have we found ourselves publicly agreeing to a statement while privately disagreeing so as not to rock the boat? How many of us have stopped ourselves from speaking up against a popular view or withheld ourselves from stating a non-conformist idea, because we have felt this would maintain harmony within the group? How many times have we wittingly minimized conflict to maximize cohesiveness? How many times have we been involved in decisions where we reached a consensus without critically testing or evaluating the ideas put forth? How many times have we not taken advantage of the benefits of working together and comfortably slipped into groupthink? How many times have we chosen to go along with something in order to get along? How many times have we preferred getting along for the sake of time and to avoid conflict? How many times have we inhibited discussions in order to avoid disagreement and/or presented a united front because we have been overly concerned in reaching an agreement?

Your responses to many of the preceding questions may be similar to mine: far too often! If so, you likely understand how debilitating groupthink can be on the quality of work that takes place when groups function this way. Discovering and implementing appropriate responses to these dilemmas is key to successfully minimizing groupthink.

Vigilant Thinking that Fosters Quality Decisions and Reduces Groupthink

- Develop a group structure that encourages quality decisions.
- Encourage disagreement and seek out differences of opinion.
- Actively seek out minority views.
- Surround yourself with different and opposing viewpoints.
- Consider the merits of a suggestion not the status of the person making the suggestion.
- Separate the process of generating ideas from evaluating them.
- Be critical of ideas not people.
- When contributing your commitment and/or approval to each and every decision in
  your team, first harken back to the "I" versus "We" statement of "how do I differentiate between what I need to 'let go of' in service of the team and what do I need 'to hold onto' in service of the team?"

PERSONAL NOTES

REFERENCES

Adair, J. (1988). *The action centred leader.* London: The Industrial Society.

Anderson, J. (1985). Working with groups: Little known facts that challenge well known myths. *Small Group Behavior, 16* (3) 267-283.

Bales, R. F. (1950). *Interaction process analysis: A method for the study of small groups.* Cambridge, Mass.: Addison-Wesley.

Beebe, S.A., & Masterson, J. L. (2003). *Communicating in Small Groups.* New York: Pearson Education Inc.

Blake, R. R. and Mouton, J. S. (1985). "Don't let group norms stifle creativity." *Personnel, 62, No. 8,* 28-33

Clarkson, P. (1999). Group image and the stages of group development. *Transitional Analysis Journal, 21,* 36 - 50.

Corsini, R.J. (1957). *Methods of Group Psychotherapy.* New York: McGraw-Hill.

Covey, S. (1989) *The seven habits of highly effective people.* New York: Simon and Schuster.

Diener, E. (1980). Deindividuation: The absence of self-awareness and self-regulation in group members. In P. B. Paulus (Ed.), *Psychology of group influence.* Hillsdale, NJ: Erlbaum.

Dimock, H.G. (1987). *Groups: Leadership and group development.* San Diego: University Associates.

Dimock, H.G. (1993). *How to observe your group.* (3rd ed.) North York: Captus Press Inc.

Dimock, H.G. and Devine, I. (1994). *Making work groups effective, (3rd ed.)* North York: Captus Press Inc.

Dubrin, A. (2001). *Leadership. (3rd ed.)* New York: Houghton Mifflin Co.

Durkin, H. (1964). *The group in depth.* New York: International Universities Press Inc.

Hackman, J. R. (1987). The design of work teams. In J. W. Lorsch (Ed.), *Handbook of organizational behaviour.* Englewood cliffs, NJ: Prentice Hall.

Harris, T. E. & Sherblom, J. (2005). *Small group and team communication.* Toronto: Allyn & Bacon.

Hearn, G. (1957). A process of group development. Autonomous Groups Bulletin, 13, 1-7.

Hill, W. F. & Gruner, L. (1973). A study of development in open and closed groups. *Small Group Behavior, 4,* 355-381.

Janis, I. (1971). *Groupthink. Psychology Today, 5 (6)*, 43-46, 74-76.

Janis, I. (1972). *Victims of groupthink.* Boston: Houghton & Mifflin.

Janis, I. (1982). *Groupthink.* Boston: Houghton & Mifflin.

Johnson, D.W., Johnson, R., & Holubec, E. (1998a). *Cooperation in the classroom. (*7th ed.*)* Edina, MN: Interaction Book Company.

Johnson, D.W., Johnson, R. & Holubec, E. (1998b). Advanced Cooperative Learning (5th ed.) Edina, MN: Interaction Book Company.

Johnson, D.W. & Johnson, R. (2003). Joining together: Group theory and group skills. (8th ed.) New York: Pearson Education Inc.

Lewin, K. (1943). Dynamics of group action. *Educational Leadership, 1*, 195-200.

Lichtman, R. J. and Lane, I. M. (1983). "Effects of group norms and goal setting on productivity." *Group and Organization Studies, 8*, No. 4, 406-420.

Lumsden, G. & Lumsden, D. (2000). *Communicating in groups and teams.* Canada: Wadsworth.

Martin, E.A. & Hill, W.F. (1957) Towards a theory of group development: Six phases of therapy group development. *International Journal of Psychotherapy,* 7, 20 - 30

Maples, M.F. (1988). Group Development: Extending Tuckman's theory. *Journal for Specialists in Group Work,* 13, 17 - 23.

Moosbruker, J. (1987). Using a stage theory model to understand and manage group dynamics. In W.B. Reddy and C. Henderson Jr. (Eds). *Training theory and practice.* Arlington, VA: N.T.L. Institute for Applied Behavioral Science.

Mosvick, R.K. & Nelson, R. B. (1987). *We've got to start meeting like this!* Glenview, IL: Scott Florsham

Napier, R.W. & Gershenfeld, M.K. (1999). Groups: *Theory and practice (6th ed).* Boston: Houghton Mifflin Company

Nick, C. *Medicine for the mind: Healing words to help you soar.* New York: McGraw Hill, 1995.

Rioch, M.J. (1970). The work of Wilfred Bion on groups. *Psychiatry, 33,* 56 - 66.

Rothwell, J.D. (2004). *In mixed company (5th ed.)* Canada: Thomson Wadsworth Inc.

Smith, K. & Berg, D.N. (1987). A paradoxical conception of group dynamics. *Journal of Human Relations, 40,* 633-658.

Sorenson, S. (May 1981). *"Group Hate"* paper presented at the International Communication Association: Mineapolis, Minnesota.

Tuckman, B.W. & Jenson, M.A. (1977) Stages of group development revisited. *Group and Organization Studies, 2,* 419-427.

Tuckman, B.W. (1965). Developmental sequence in small groups. *Psychological Bulletin, 63, (6),* 384 - 399.

Van Ekeren, G. (1988). *The speaker's source book.* Englewood Cliffs, NJ: Prentice Hall.

Wilson, G.L. & Hanna, M.S. (1993) *Groups in Context. (3rd ed.)* New York: McGraw-Hill.

SECTION III

EMERGENT UNDERSTANDING
OF EFFECTIVE GROUPS

"I don't want to go among mad people," said Alice.
"Oh, you can't help that," said the cat.
"We're all mad here."

-Lewis Carroll

I. TEAM INVOLVEMENT AND TASK ACCOMPLISHMENT IN OUR DIGITAL AGE: THE GOOD, THE BAD, AND THE UGLY

As a faculty member in a graduate school that subscribes to semi-virtual teams to accomplish i program, I have begun to notice how the evolution of technology is influencing teamwork and tas performance.

Context: Semi-Virtual Teams in a Graduate Program

Students in our graduate program come from across Canada, with a sprinkle from North America, Sou American, Europe, Asia, and Africa. Approximately 40-50 percent are from outside of Quebec where th university is situated. Professions range from the health and educational sectors, government, social an community services, and public and private organizations. Age range is between 24 and 55 year Students move through their program as a cohort, meeting once a month for three days, with the bulk c their teamwork and group support done interdependently through e-mail, Skype, teleconferenceing computer conferencing, electronic voting, doodle polls (polling members' ideas, opinions, weighting and judgments), text messaging, and online databases that provide information and maintai communication.

Sounds great- but is it? Despite all this emphasis on collaborating teamwork and communicatio technology aimed at facilitating and supporting a team in action, it is not uncommon that, by the tim the cohort reaches their studies in their second year, trust is low, individual and group accountabilit fragile, and commitment to working as a team, while seen as a necessary feature, is not welcomed. Wh is this so?

The Digital Village

There is no question that this innovative graduate program would not have been possibl without the technology that supports it. Many of the graduates experience themselves in a digital villag where they are able to access and transmit data quickly without delays imposed by geographica distance. The use of technology is not a problem, for many have not lived in a world without the Internet.

Semi-Virtual Teams Virtually Break Down

During the first six weeks following the residential lab experience has usually been on the task. The digital village is abuzz. E-mails fly back and forth, ideas abound, and suggestions are exchanged. The pace is quick and enthusiasm is high. As the work becomes more complex, different individuals push for decisions, others push to keep things open, and still others for more time to do research. Misunderstandings begin to appear blame begins to spread, and feedback, although sought after, is resisted, ignored, or rejected unless it subscribes to the persons perspective. Conference calls diminish in frequency and when they do take place are often perfunctory, with the usual check –ins eliminated in the service of time.

With the focus solely directed towards the task, communication begins to be dominated by a few members relaying directives of decisions unilaterally made. "Flaming"- a sort of e-mail bashing or "water cooler" syndrome- begins to appear with individuals starting to talk negatively about their peers. This leads to "bad blood" and, in some cases, open hostility. Subgroups take over often failing to keep others informed, while still others begin to feel ignored and/or left out.

Lessons Learned

While we have generally managed to work through areas that impact the students' work during the weekend, there are many lessons to be derived from this repeated scenario where a group's productivity, consequently the project productivity, has dropped considerably because of the limitations the group was under.

These graduate students are busy professional who work hard in their personal, professional, and academic lives. They take their studies seriously and are interested in what they do. They have worked hard during the six weeks with a deep desire to do well and deliver.

II. POLARITY IMBALANCE: THE TYRANNY OF THE "OR"

During the six weeks between the lab and the students' team intervention, as the work becomes more complex and the task focus intensifies, the initial attempt to balance task with maintenance quickly drops to the point of being non-existent. With the continued absence of maintenance, work level begins to drop, interest level begins to wane, and the collective begins to fragment, with the interdependence initially experienced and sought after breaking down. Teams begin to work independently, often at odds with each other with subgroups within teams isolating themselves even further.

Balance of task and maintenance is difficult at the best of times, but is paramount when team members are working on an interdependent project and living in different geographic places. Understanding that task and maintenance are one unit with polarities that nourish the other rather than opposing forces is difficult, but it is even more difficult to understand and manage in a digital world. Task and maintenance represent opposing but complementary forces in our lives. When the parts are in opposition, energy is not freely available to flow. The complementary is only manifested when the conflict disappears. The challenge is letting go of the tyranny of the "or" and learning how to integrate the poles in order to move forward and create an environment ready for decision making and supportive actions. In other words, to gain and maintain the benefits of one pole, one must also be able to pursue the benefits of the other and be able to embrace both extremes at the same time, instead of choosing between A and B. Participants must figure out a way to have both A and B and view these polarities as interdependent, something to be managed, not as a problem to be solved (Johnson, 1996).

Delegation with Trust: Stepping into a Universe of Possibility

The lowering of trust has been a chronic problem in semi-virtual teams that are composed of individuals, subgroups, and/or volunteer teams who are mandated to work on an aspect of a project. The cycle is familiar. A subgroup (person) volunteers to work on a piece of a larger project. Pitfall number one: the mandate is unclear. Pitfall number two: the mandate does not get clarified and the subgroup (person) proceeds to work on the task. They send in their work, e-mails are exchanged, discussion or disagreements ensue, the task is re-assigned or taken over by another subgroup or person, and the work gets redone. There is an atmosphere of discontent and the seeds of resentment begin to grow. Everyone is upset.

The cycle can take on another variation. A subgroup (person) volunteers or is assigned a piece of a larger project. The mandate is clear and the subgroup (person) proceeds to work on the task. They send in their work, they are thanked, and, without their knowing, the task is re-assigned or taken over by another subgroup or person, and the work gets redone. Discontent, resentment, and misunderstandings follow. Everyone is unhappy. When this cycle repeats itself, a state of mistrust gets fostered, involvement lowers, resistance grows; and when volunteers are needed for another task, they are either not forthcoming, or the task gets picked up with reluctance and/or noncompliance. This mistrust—fear cycle constrains and is self-fulfilling. There is preoccupation with boundary-setting and protecting one's turf and the development of protective pairing; collusion and subgrouping begins to emerge. Work gets undertaken with a sense of duty and with little interest or investment.

I have seen this painful cycle in many non-virtual teams. However, the extent to which this occurs in semi-virtual teams is much more frequent. I might add alarmingly so. Once again, I have puzzled about this. As I listen to the power issues experienced, the misunderstandings, and the hostilities that emerge under such circumstances, I am left with the impression that it is easier to dismiss another person's work (in this case a peer) when the encounter and decision taken is not face-to-face.

While Gibb (1972) talks about "learning to trust one's mistrust", he also talks about how the presence of trust provides an environment that nourishes personal growth and unleashes potential, while fear and anger take it away. While no one can program the development of trust in a team, let alone in a semi-virtual team, trusting that what has been delegated will be undertaken with a search for excellence nurtures the development of a supportive atmosphere and helps to narrow the gap between what is expressed and what is wanted. This is not to say that everything that gets mandated will be done with a view to excellence, but what it does suggest is that trust with delegation paves the way for sharing relevant concerns and allows for data to flow, facilitating healthy decision making and sound choices.

Accountability: A Retreat from Mediocrity

Setting norms that encourage standards of accountability within a team is challenging at the best of times. Instilling accountability as a primary mechanism within semi-virtual teams is even more challenging for non-face-to-face interactions. The person is not in front of you, only the person's work. For many, the easier path is to avoid being transparent and write a perfunctory note of thanks and then stew.

Avoidance or absence of accountability creates resentment among team members who have different standards of performance. Missing deadlines and key deliverables, distributing incomplete work, and/or being unavailable foster deterioration of relationships, encourage mediocrity, and lower commitment. Both the product and the relationship deteriorate.

There is much irony in this vicious cycle. Often team members do not want to call their peers on performance or behaviors for fear this might hurt the individual or jeopardize the relationship. The very thing they want to avoid invariably occurs. The relationship does deteriorate. As lower standards prevail, dysfunctional team behavior appears and the team begins to stagnate and fails to grow.

The most effective and efficient means of maintaining high standards of performance on a team is peer pressure. When a team holds one another accountable, it establishes respect among team members who are held to the same high standards. It also enables potential problems to be identified by questioning one another's approaches without hesitation.

The Power of the Narrative: Learning from the Inside Out

The following excerpts are from two of my graduate students illustrating the struggle and appreciation of technology and how this influenced their teamwork. While they were in the same program, they were in different years.

⚑   Louise

We left our lab on a high. We seemed to have pulled together as a team more so than any of us would have hoped, given the trials and tribulations we had encountered in our group work over the previous year. We had creatively come up with a vision for the workshop we were going to design, and had rallied around the principles that were to guide our work.

However, after having shared a full week of residential experience, we now had to disperse into the outside world, to our full-time jobs and families and find the time to connect with the two subgroups each of us was a part of for the design and logistical preparation of the workshop.

There were three of us in my design team and all lived close by. So we tackled our work through three face-to-face meetings and a few e-mails. My logistics team was larger with six participants spread across four cities. Our meetings were held on Skype and we used e-mail for follow-up.

Our first hurdle was to find an appropriate time for our conference calls. Negotiating one person's commitment on Mondays, another person's unavailability but Monday and Wednesdays, parents in the group wanting to talk after kids went to bed, and one person being in a different time zone left us with Wednesday evenings at nine as the only possible option. This meant 10 p.m. for the person living in the Maritimes. The lateness of the hour was a challenge because calls would start with everyone a bit tired from their days and focused mainly on the call being over in no more than an hour. I believe the time constraints that we accept as a consequence of having a virtual team affect our capacity to appropriately deal with maintenance as we focus on the task at hand.. An additional difficulty of Skype calling, or any teleconferencing for that matter, is the unnatural flow of conversation. People must speak in sequence to be heard; a person trying to interject into someone else's comment is usually not heard by the initial speaker so that everyone else can hear them talking over each other in a confused deaf dialogue. Inevitably as this happens, a third individual chimes in, in an effort to make them aware of the overlap, creating only further confusion. With everyone vying for efficient conversation, this waste of time becomes irritating.

Each week when the hour was up, some people pressed for more time to finalize the decisions being made, while others advocated that we respect our time engagements. In between phone calls and e-mails, Google posts were used so that people could share with the group whatever portions of the work they had been assigned to do. Of course, here again some inefficiencies occurred. Not everyone consulted their e-mails or the posted documents in a timely fashion and the group had to negotiate through more e-mails, whether to wait for them or make decisions and move on. The task-focused people wanted to move on, the maintenance-focused ones wanted all-around inclusion.

In other words, while the technology allows virtual teams to tackle their work, it puts an additional burden on the already complex feat of managing a group's process. It particularly affects the group's ability to attend to maintenance. Not enough time is set aside for this and the context creates additional irritants that polarize the result-driven people from the process driven people.

ACTION STEPS WHEN WORKING IN SEMI-VIRTUAL AND VIRTUAL TEAMS

FOCUS ON THE BIG PICTURE:

The old adage it is hard to see the big picture when you are inside the frame" applies here. Sub-teams need to know how their work contributes to the whole and benefits the client system they are serving. Where possible, decide on a minimum of one face-to-face meeting to get the big picture, understand flow, and physically meet and connect with each other

SET PRIORITIES AND REVIEW THEM FREQUENTLY:

This helps navigate your way through setbacks, misdirection, and cynics who set the team's emotional tone

CREATE A STRONG FEEDBACK AND LEARNING LOOP:

Team members need to regularly reflect on what they should keep, stop doing, and start doing. This needs to be shared with an exchange of feedback for reality testing.

CREATE GROUP-DECISION WORK TEAMS:

These GD Work Teams would be aimed at reducing some of the technological barriers to collaborative group work, such as unequal consideration of ideas, dominance of individuals, peer pressure, and loss of autonomy.

HOLD TEAM MEMBERS ACCOUNTABLE FOR THEIR WORK:

Expectations need to be clarified and feedback given with clarity and support. Where necessary, joint problem solving of the issue at hand needs to be done.

CELEBRATE, CELEBRATE, CELEBRATE:

Look for opportunities to celebrate the team's successes and milestones that have been covered, and projects that have been completed.

FIGURE X-1

▷ **Richard**

Since we were all in different locations, it was agreed that we would use telephone conference calls as the means to connect. Planning the effective use of technology and giving structure to it was extremely helpful. Why telephone conference calls? In the first year, a number of us had tried team meetings for different projects using Internet-based programs such as Gizmo and Skype. The experience was less than satisfactory; there was often interference on the line, which seemed to get worse with the number of people on the conference call. A lesson learned here on the use of technology was not to stick with something that was not working.

We then tried a telephone tag system, whereby one person would call another, the other then initiated a three-way call with another, and we were able to connect the four or five team members in this telephone link. The quality was good, and those who made the long distance connections already were on unlimited long distance plans so there was no added cost to any of the participants. This became our means of team meetings. For the most part, it also provided the added capacity of being able to talk by phone and then have our computers with Internet connection up and running at the same time. This that during the meeting, we could forward documents to each other and have everyone looking at the relevant documents and providing feed-back on the call.

In between telephone conferences, technology also played an important role, as e-mail was used to exchange documents and provide needed written material, instructions, and clarifications. Although technology became a key tool in our work together, tele-phone meetings and e-mail exchanges were not enough. The use of technology had its limits in terms of being able to see and feel the big picture. Although the parts each team worked on seemed to make sense, the technology or our use of it did not allow us to get a sense of the flow of the workshop and how each session would feel and fit.

We decided to meet face-to-face to see how everybody's work fitted together. The coming together was an important learning because it did point out some major challenges in the workshop's design and flow that we were able to adjust as a result. We needed to see and feel the design in action. We needed to see and talk to each other about the design face-to-face. People had worked hard on their own pieces and had to go through this process of being together — seeing the design in action and providing feedback for some people to let go of some of the work they had done in service of the client and the team — so that they could recommit to redesign. Some of the pitfalls of the telephone chain system and similar computer-based telephone conference options is that we were not able to see the verbal cues of the other.

(Next Page) ━ ━ ━ ━ ━ ━ ━ ━ ━ ━ ━ ━ ━ ━ ➤

This meant providing timely and critical feedback was difficult to some. In one of the teams I was part of, I was having a problem with a member who I felt was not fully committed to our work. This person would never step up and volunteer to take minutes or produce documents and was even absent for one or two of our meetings. I only addressed this when I was face-to-face with the person and by then our team's work had been completed.

As I reflect back on this, I question whether technology can be used as a means by some who are fully committed to go along with the team, but not pull their weight. Technology was an essential tool in our cohort's work together over the six weeks before meeting our client. It enabled us to continue our work and deal with the many facets of putting together a workshop. It alone was not enough, however. We needed face-to-face time to check in and get a feel for the design by actually seeing it and feeling it. Technology, like any tool, can truly help teams do good work together. Knowing the limits of the tool is essential, however, when planning how to use it effectively and efficiently.

Replenishing Our Human Moments: A Challenge Worth Exploring

Several things stand out for me as I reflect on my observations, the experiences of my graduate students, and the personal narratives that have been written capture the experience of many. They help us understand the influence of technology on virtual and semi-virtual teams first-hand.

Technology Is Here to Stay

While technology is here to stay, it is still too early to determine and understand its long-term impact on collaborative work, quality decision-making, and sustained commitment to the task at hand. The importance of understanding this influence cannot be underscored sufficiently. In so doing we would be better able to build interventions to facilitate the important work that could, should, and will be done by semi-virtual and virtual teams in our future world of today.

COMMON CONCERNS, PITFALLS, AND DIFFICULTIES EXPERIENCED IN VIRTUAL AND SEMI-VIRTUAL TEAMS

1. Support fades when most needed.
2. Teleconferencing creates an unnatural flow of conversation and becomes a disconnected experience.
3. Difficulty negotiating phone calls with different geographic time zones.
4. Focus on big picture lost as teams work on parts.
5. Subgroupings emerge with those working side-by-side.
6. E-mail experience riddled with misunderstandings and emotionality.
7. Trust lowers as technology is allowed to take over.
8. Decision-making structure unclear and not agreed upon.
9. Skills and expertise not used maximally, and in some cases not at all.
10. Mandates are ambiguous and/or unrealistic.
11. Peers not held accountable for deliverables.
12. Technological capacity allows knowing each other only through task.

FIGURE X-2

What we do know is that the use of technology brings us into a paperless world that is both archival and efficient, permitting meetings without travel. File systems make it possible to re-display information from previous meetings, to revisit old arguments, to show history of a series of arguments, and to resume discussions. My graduate students report that when the text includes graphics and is clear, concise, and consistent in spelling and grammar, and affirming in tone, it has a positive impact, particularly when there is a request, critiquing a piece of someone's else's work or giving a rationale on an action to be taken. They also state that it is experienced negatively when messages are curt and boorish and fail to get their point across to accomplish goals or advances in strategies. Their observations speak volumes and need to be explored further. The following action steps can be followed if common pitfalls and difficulties experienced in virtual and semi virtual teams do occur:

ACTION STEP 1:

Establish maintenance norms

Set up a prearranged structure that allows for three brief processing periods:
a)   Brief check-in as the team starts their conference call
b)   Halfway stop and check how peers are experiencing the meeting
c)   Closure check-in as to how the team experienced the meeting and what to watch out for the next time
d)   In addition, summarize activities to be taken and ensure follow through.

ACTION STEP 2:

Agree on ground rules

The team needs to agree and commit to ground rules for making decisions, resolving disagreements, debating issues, etc. Anyone overstepping these ground rules needs to be called on it by team members.

ACTION STEP 3:

Assess and adjust your meeting process

ACTION STEP 4:
Give opportunity to vent but not blame

Encourage the team to vent and air their frustrations. However, you need to monitor when it slips into blame, gossip, and gets off tangent.

ACTION STEP 5:
Redirect discussions not involving all team members

When discussion involve some but not all team members, redirect and encourage those involved to discuss the issue at hand.

III. EMOTIONAL INTELLIGENCE: THE OTHER SIDE OF BEING SMART

In the fast lane of business life today, people spend more time on computer keyboards, BlackBerries, and conference calls than they do in face-to-face communication. We're expected to piece together broken conversations, cryptic voice mails, and abbreviated text messages to figure out how to proceed. In this increasingly complex web, emotional intelligence is more important than ever before.

— Rajeev Peshawaria,
Executive Director
Goldman Sachs International

What is emotional intelligence (E.Q.)? Why is it getting so much attention these days? What role does it play in the development of effective workgroups? What role does it play in our lives as we become students in our university system, as we enter the workforce, and/or as we give leadership to work teams that need to produce and perform under pressure? Why is it that the intellect cannot work at its best without E.Q.? Why is it that people with high I.Q. often flounder and those with modest E.Q. flourish?

The human body has two brains and two different kinds of intelligence, say scientists: the rational brain and the emotional brain, which control how we think and how we act. Like Siamese twins, the body's brains in the head and the gut are interconnected; when one gets upset, the other does too. The emotional brain can take over the thinking brain and paralyze it when it is feeling anxiety or distress. These two intelligences are quite different. While I.Q. is important, it is not everything. At best it contributes only 20 percent to the factors that determine life success. Even among talented pools of high I.Q. people, the most valued are those who can cooperate, collaborate, listen, support, empathize with others, and build consensus. It is not that I.Q. skills are irrelevant. On the contrary, they do matter, but mainly as "threshold capabilities" (Goleman, 1998b).

All very well, but what does all this mean? What does emotional intelligence have to do with making workgroups more effective? Why is it so important? Emotional intelligence is crucial for workgroups for it is the essential ingredient that fosters a healthy, productive workgroup environment. An emotionally intelligent group is able to create an environment in which members value their membership, collaboratively focus on what needs to be done, and address issues that need to be dealt with. In short, it has everything to do with sustainability and transferability.

A few words about emotional intelligence: these are "portable skills" that can be acquired by anyone. They develop when we are open to learning and when we are open to feedback from others. They require practice, reflection, and the discipline of noticing. In other words, you have to work for it and be vigilant in its practice for any benefits to be reaped, for it diminishes in impact and value when it gets no outdoor exercise.

Central to emotional intelligence is self-awareness and self-regulation. In other words, emotional intelligence is being aware of one's emotions and knowing how to regulate and manage them. These two sets of competencies are directed both inward toward self and outward toward managing others. They are complex, yet simple. The framework in Figure 13 captures Daniel Goleman's (1998a) four pillars of emotional intelligence: self-assessment, self-management, social awareness, and relationship management.

GOLEMAN'S FOUR PILLARS OF EQ
FIGURE X-4

Emotional intelligence is the product of two sets of skills: personal and social competence.

In the next few pages, we will examine some of the growing "illiteracy" of emotional intelligence and some factors influencing this trend, with examples of what we see in the university today and its impact on

Emotional Intelligence Skill Areas	Emotional Awareness Abilities	Emotional Management Abilities
Personal Competence	Self-Awareness of one's **own** emotions	Self-Management (Self-Regulation) of one's **own** emotions
Social Competence	Social Awareness of **others'** emotions	Relationship Management of **others'** emotions

workgroups and the experience and struggle of a very bright person involved in groups, who has woken up to the fact that I.Q. can only "get you so far". Some perceived E.Q. essentials for the development of an effective, healthy group community are identified in an orbiting space station with an international multicultural crew. Concrete action steps for developing and sustaining a team's emotional intelligence will then be discussed.

The New Yardstick of Today

"We're being judged by a new yardstick: not just by how smart we are, or by our training and expertise, but also by how well we handle ourselves and each other" (Goleman, 1998a). We are entering a new era in our world today, where emotional intelligence — the ability to get along with people and make good decisions — is more important to life's success than the academic intelligence measured in I.Q. tests. While an individual's emotional quotient cannot be underscored sufficiently, it is becoming apparent that a groups' E.Q. may be even more important in our world today where most of our work gets done. In fact, it is rare to see an organizational system today that does not rely on teams to accomplish its tasks and produce results. Work in isolation today is relatively rare, while work in relationship to others has become the norm. Teams that learn to function in emotionally intelligent ways remain vital and dynamic in the competitive marketplace of today.

Over the past years, I have been painfully aware that I am faced with an increasing number of students demonstrating emotional ineptitude and struggling with illiteracy about emotional intelligence. This is a remarkable observation as our department places a strong emphasis on areas such as self-awareness, empathy, and interpersonal relations, the importance of teamwork and collaborative decision-making, and the immeasurable value of maximizing team effectiveness and leadership development through the use of field practicums, internships, and facilitation of small groups. While every attempt is made to enhance the effectiveness of work teams, we seem to be producing more dysfunctional teams than our former vibrant, creative, and productive ones. This new trend is disturbing, for it is growing. Why is this so?

Plugged In, But Tuned out

Technology — cell phones, iPods, BlackBerry cells, laptops, notebooks, online Moodle, online courses, distance learning, video-conference learning, texting, automated phone directory, etc. — used widely with our students today colors much of their social interaction.

Our current culture of efficiency over effectiveness — online course evaluations, search engines used for primary sources, the "just Google" lifestyle mentality, multi-tasking (music + TV + cell) while working on assignments with language used by students incongruent with university-level standards is driving academic requirements to an all-time low.

We have 24-hour coffee shops where wireless Internet turns night into day, background noise at bars that discourages interaction (cigarette smokers build the real connections due to less noise, fewer people when outside, combined with a commonality), and an increase in people eating out, but with little to no conversation during this activity. We see the rise in boredom in our schools with a decrease of its opposite —engagement and interest — with kids nodding off, or texting their friends, or disappearing into their own thoughts. Age differences that used to be so complementary in the universities, resulting in rich exchange of knowledge and experience, is now not the case. Older students are seen as "odd" by younger students and academic standards have been lowered.

The routine in class these days starts with "please turn off your cells". This leads students to text messaging. They have become very adept at texting without looking at their cell phone keyboard. Now the announcement goes further: "please turn off your cells and no text messaging". This does not work either. The vibrating gadget connected with cell phones allows anyone to know someone has called. A light or flashing light informs the receiver that an e-mail has just come in. Students desperately resort to creative ways of trying to instantly access these messages. Despite feedback, they get caught up in a world of their own, where their self-awareness is dulled and their self-regulation is seemingly non-existent.

This culture of the *now* — where we need it now, quickly, this instant produces students who send e-mails and expect an answer instantaneously, who display a "why bother with Facebook" attitude when replies on Twitter are so much more immediate, and who do not bother with CDs and DVDs anymore, because a download of iTunes means "I don't have to get off my couch", and so on. As we lose all ability to wait, patience isn't so much a virtue as an annoyance, epitomized by the fact some even text while driving.

The implications of these trends on sustaining and building effective workgroups are enormous. The basis and foundation for good group work seems to have weakened. Building relationships and mutual trust among group members has become increasingly difficult with dialogue harder to maintain and sharing of relevant task concerns more difficult to address. There seems to be little to no interest in engaging in interpersonal understanding and regulating the group's emotions. I have seen teams spend more time interacting with their screens than with each other. They miss cues, tone of voice, rolling of eyes, fidgeting, and non-verbal behaviors that occur. They also miss the impact of their own actions on their teammates. With time, accountability and willingness to take on responsibility seems to be harder to sustain, loyalty suffers, and workgroups, when assigned a task, find it exhausting and difficult to engage in meaningful and interdependent ways where resources and skills are recognized and valued.

With inadequate conditions prevailing and the development of effective task processes not in evidence, it is understandable why workgroups struggle and become dysfunctional, why the quality of the task begins to suffer, and why members experience relief when their work and the group is finally over.

Balancing and Managing Team Emotional Intelligence: The Heart of the Matter

> *The Whole Image of a Man in America today is: "You can't feel."*
> *I say "Goddam it, let me feel."*
>
> -   *A Vietnam Veteran*

Teams are cauldrons of bubbling emotions. Anyone who has worked in a team noted the inescapable influence of a group's emotional underworld. Anyone who has been a member of a task group experienced the swing in shifts in the work level of a group when the emotional level of the group had not been taken care of (Kass, 2008). On an average, we experience 27 emotions each waking hour. With nearly 17 waking hours in a day, we are likely to experience throughout the day about 459 emotional experiences. If one does the math, more than 3,200 emotions guide us through the week, and more than 170,000 each year. These are astonishing numbers and underscore the importance of building and nurturing a team's emotional intelligence, particularly as most of these emotions will occur during working hours. These are also indicative of the importance of developing and using the "portable skills" of emotional intelligence in work teams whether on earth, in extreme isolation, or in space.

As a university professor in a department of applied human sciences, one of the courses I teach is an undergraduate course in small group behavior. I have taught this course for a good number of years and have observed the growing illiteracy of team emotional intelligence. I

The following two episodes, one at the undergraduate level and one at the graduate level, illustrate this growing trend.

Inclusion Turns Out to Be Exclusion: Whatever Happened to Member Needs?

In my undergraduate course on leadership, I use a three-hour teach-in/fishbowl process — a process that involves group presentation and group observation. The process often results in a powerful experience for both the presenting group and those watching the experience unfold.

The Context: During the second term of this undergraduate course on leadership in task groups, the class is divided in symposium teams, each becoming responsible for a central group dynamic focus. Areas typically chosen are decision-making, leadership, power and influence, diversity, and norms. Following their choices, each member is further asked to choose a group dynamic perspective with the aim of exploring and linking it to their team's main symposium focus. These perspectives are drawn from a long list, such as conflict, gender, roles, group development, hidden agendas, E.Q., humor, membership, groupthink, etc. Students are given several weeks to prepare and present their focus and their perspectives to the class in the form of an experiential teach-in. Following their presentation, each presenting group is asked to sit in a "fishbowl", in which I also join. The focus of the "fishbowl" is to understand their process, how they worked together, and how they made decisions. The rest of the class form the outer circle, observe, listen, and halfway through I invite them to share their observations and insights.

The Incident: This particular symposium team had as their main focus "Power and Influence". The team consisted of seven members. Their chosen perspectives were gender, conflict, membership, E.Q., hidden agendas, and group development. Fairly quickly into their presentation, it became evident that there were serious unresolved team issues and that these issues impacted both the quality and product of their work. It was painful to watch.

As the fishbowl progressed, it became evident that there had been very poor inclusion of certain members, to the point of deliberate exclusion, and that destructive norms had been nurtured allowing for no perspective taking, no room for interpersonal understanding or commitment to building the team. There was no effort made to dealing with emotions that were surfacing, which were regularly being suppressed by the more powerful and vocal members who controlled the group's process, and all the while justifying their actions in service of the work that needed to be done.

What became evident was that the topic they were studying and presenting to the class had only impacted them intellectually. Their actions bore no relation to their words. The group's emotional intelligence seemed shaky. Their ability or desire to regulate and work with their group's emotions was missing. More stunning was the absence of group awareness of the emotional havoc that was being sewn as the group went about preparing for their task. When I ventured to ask the member who had studied membership and had presented his section with great skill whether he saw a relationship between his perspective and the inclusion and the subsequent development of membership in his group, he drew a blank and genuinely seemed puzzled by the question.

This is not an isolated experience. More and more groups seem disconnected with their group's process and lost in the emotional dynamics that surface. In some cases, there is self-awareness and poor self-regulation; in others, there is no group self-awareness and no self-regulation; and in most groups, there seems to be a lack of structure that allows effective task processes to emerge.

Espoused Theory versus Theory in Use: Now You See It, Now You Don't

In a graduate course I recently taught, students spent time studying, designing, planning, and eventually implementing a workshop on emotional intelligence to an outside organization. They were a very bright group of professionals, skilled in their field, experienced in working on project teams and task groups, and knew their data.

The Context: It became evident, as I worked with them and as I watched them work with the outside system, that they had developed counter-productive norms of self-regulating as a team. While they stressed the

---

POINTERS, HIGHLIGHTS, AND KEY FEATURES FOR AN EFFECTIVE HEALTHY GROUP

1. Teams operate on two levels: work and emotional.
2. Technology today colors most of our social interaction, shifting the basis and foundation of norm development within work teams.
3. Quality of teamwork suffers when members lack emotional intelligence.
4. Collective emotional intelligence is complicated, as a team needs to attend to both the relationship management of its members and the group as a whole.
5. Team self-awareness does not automatically lead to team self-regulation.
6. Team suppression of discontent and frustration is counter to healthy team self-regulation.
7. Perspective-taking nourishes the building of team emotional intelligence.
8. Structures that allow emotional dialogue to surface also increase participation and collaboration among members.
9. Team performance increases when members recognize and acknowledge the emotions that surface and influence their work.
10. Team relationship management paves the way for healthy group communication with other workgroups within and outside of the organization.

FIGURE X-5

---

importance of a group's emotional intelligence to their clients, and the vital importance of handling a group's emotional level, they ironically did the reverse of what they espoused. I noted that they tended to suppress expressions of discontent and frustration arising between peers unless it was directed toward authority figures. They had developed ways of smoothing things over, unwittingly nourishing an environment that lacked safety and freedom of expression, and an environment in which feedback was limited and issues that needed to be dealt with were ignored, or brushed aside. They had difficulty balancing support with confrontation, and the fine line between concern and control often was blurred. When interpersonal or group issues surfaced with occasional outbursts of anger, they were either greeted with silence and "business as usual" or members withdrawing and pouting. On the surface, the group seemed competent, open, and focused.

Choice to Wear Blinders: Before working with the client, the cohort was challenged to focus and study their own emotional intelligence. It became clear that while they had skills to address this as a topic on an intellectual basis, they had difficulty looking at it on a more personal basis. Their resistance was such that subgroups in most cases became non-functional, and groups that moved forward were the ones that had remained open to learning from the inside-out. Their willingness to go further facilitated the development of processes dealing with task, team, and individual needs. In short, they had attended to the inescapable influence of their team's emotional underworld.

As mentioned earlier, this was a bright and hard-working group. However, their unwillingness to examine their own emotional intelligence disabled their capacity to establish norms of supportive behavior. They chose to wear blinders, resulting in groupthink with no proactive engagement in problem solving when confronted with critical issues and with no appreciation of the necessity for collaborative decision-making (Janis, 1972). When difficulties arose, they blamed circumstances or those in authority. When the course ended, the group's termination level was determined by the social networks it had formed. While termination took place, closure did not. Their choices influenced their product, contributing to their lack of understanding of the value of dealing with their group's emotional intelligence.

The Inner Rudder: Our Most Precious Resource

The following is a poignant narrative of a very special, intellectually talented individual who continues to struggle with her self-regulation. Her self-awareness does not serve as an inner rudder for her choices, thus influencing negatively her focus and her energy. I have included this narrative (with her permission) as her profile represents gifted individuals whose talent and intellect, while an asset to a group are a challenge to access and, ultimately, a challenge to the group's productivity and effectiveness.

☞ Katie

My experience as a member of groups has been quite varied, running the gamut from project groups to teaching teams. When I look back at these experiences and reflect on my role as a member, one aspect stands out: the impact of my personal emotional intelligence. The ups and downs of my ability to recognize my E.Q. have had a profound effect on my role in these groups, as well as on my personal development.

Throughout my university career, I have been privileged to work with inspiring individuals. My interaction with these individuals over the years has put into perspective the low level of E.Q. I have possessed. As a student and colleague, I strove to portray the image of a self-confident, outgoing individual. It has not been easy to recognize (after self-reflection) how lacking I am in the self-regulation, self-awareness, and motivation areas. I aim to present myself as someone who is in control of herself and her emotions, when the reality is I fluctuated greatly during the last five years. Working in groups has helped me to be able to realize my areas of development within E.Q. While it has not been an easy journey, it has been one that I feel has benefited me greatly.

My self-regulation is shaky at best. While I felt that I was successful in monitoring my reactions to situations when working in groups, the reality is that I was hiding from my emotions, not regulating them. The results of this were quite dramatic. After having portrayed myself as someone who was appropriate in her reactions, I eventually would break down crying, confusing my fellow group members and rendering myself unable to function in a group setting. My experience as a student in a pivotal third-year experiential learning course was particularly devastating, as the second semester saw my performance spiral down, resulting in a lowered performance and grade. My fellow group members were also quite angered by my actions, which not only impacted their grade but also highlighted my inability to be a true member of the group, as I had put on a "fake" face to them and my professor. While it could be said that I maintained my social skills and empathy, the reality is that these attributes were as false as the persona I presented. My empathy was too pronounced, and I made promises and comments in order to deflect the attention from my crumbling sense of self and performance capacities.

As I reflect upon this event, it also is very telling of my level of self-awareness. Although I received feedback from numerous members of my group, I refused to examine what had happened, and why it had occurred. When asked to become part of the teaching team the following year, I eagerly accepted, hoping to prove that I was in fact a "good" team member. Once again I maintained the facade. This seemed to fool no one but myself, and I suffered another breakdown at the end of this group experience. I once again refused to acknowledge what was really going on, and continued.

(Next page) ━ ━ ━ ━ ━ ━ ━ ━ ━ ━ ➔

This lack of self-awareness resulted in a new personal low, as I struggled to keep up and accomplish the tasks I had volunteered for. I evaded and outright ignored the concerns of my fellow group members, insisting that I "was fine".

My motivation also reached a new low, as I was too busy keeping up appearances to fully enjoy and engage in the work that the team was doing.

It wasn't until a very special member of the group cornered me and gave me much needed feedback. Unlike previous attempts, this normally mild-mannered individual refused to back down until I acknowledged what I was doing to myself and the group. This once again resulted in a new low for me: I was not motivated to change my actions, and my lack of self-awareness crippled me, as I was unable to self-regulate. I attempted to become more self-aware, but quickly shielded myself from the pain this self-awareness caused and once more reverted to my old ways.

This pattern continued until new members joined the teaching team and I had a heart-to-heart with the professor on the team. I credit her strength (as well as that of my team members) in being able to deliver feedback in a way that hit close to home, as well as helping me to see the impact I have on the group when I refuse to examine my behaviors and their underlying emotions. The literature will tell you that self-awareness is key to strong emotional intelligence. It saddens me to realize that while I may one day have a higher level of self-awareness, it will not be enough. While I can become aware of what I do (and do not do), the reality is that I rarely put this self-awareness into action.

Instead, I tend to once again revert back to my script and attempt to hide my sufferings. I have held teams back due to my choices and will continue to do so until I take action. While I still struggle with highs and lows, the very fact that I can write this personal narrative is heartening, as it gives me an indication of how far my self-awareness and, consequently, all areas of my E.Q. have improved. I know my areas of development, as well as the script I follow when I have hit a low. While the change is not complete, I am making the effort to stabilize and continue my upwards movement. I have a long way to go, but I am determined to continue my journey towards a stronger Emotional Intelligence.

NORMS THAT FOSTER INDIVIDUAL AND TEAM AWARENESS AND REGULATION OF EMOTIONS

Interpersonal understanding and perspective taking	Affirm, acknowledge, and reach out	Create a trusting and safe environment
Take time to understand a perspective that represents the opposite of your own.	Acknowledge contributions, work efforts, and thoughtful interventions of others.	Take time to include new members and bring them up to speed.
Check your understanding before stating your own. When you do so, share how you are feeling.	Where possible build on teammates' ideas, suggestions, and comments.	Exercise your discernment, integrity, and moral compass.
Respect differences in perspective. Periodically ask quiet members what they are thinking.	Acknowledge feedback, even If you disagree with it. Acknowledge moments of caring.	Allow for conflict to surface Acknowledge differences and misunderstandings.
Check for understanding and commitment of decisions being considered.	Provide emotional support, where needed.	Admit your mistakes and move on.
Acknowledge your disagreement with issues being discussed.	Listen, listen, listen.	Avoid blaming, shaming, and/or gossiping about absent members.
Acknowledge your observations, if you sense unresolved undertones		Focus on problem solving, not blaming.

Surface team members' skills, hidden talents, and resources

Take time to understand the range of expertise in the group and, where possible, affirm and maximize these resources.

Acknowledge when you can't comprehend what Is going on or when you feel inadequate to the task.

Follow through with commitments and responsibilities you have chosen to take on or that has been delegated to you.

Do not say "yes" to doing something when you want to say "no", or when you have no intention of doing it.

Ask for help when you need it.

NORMS THAT FOSTER INDIVIDUAL AND TEAM AWARENESS AND REGULATION OF EMOTIONS (CONT'D)

Transfer-in	Mid-process check	Transfer-out
Start meetings with a transfer-in. This means checking in with each person as to how he or she is doing. This needs to be done regularly. This does not need to take much time, but enough time needs to be given so that each person feels heard. Listen and take into account what is being shared because it may color the emotional tone and energy in the meeting. Do not turn a transfer-in into a personal problem solving session.	Regularly structure a mid-process check-in giving members an opportunity to state their observations and feelings of how the meeting is progressing. Listen to what is being said and redirect the process or direction, where necessary.	End each meeting with a check-out. This Is very important as this will give members a sense of how each member experienced the group's productivity. This will also help members understand the group's level of task involvement and emotional investment.

FIGURE X-6

IV. DIVERSITY IS A FACT — AND A VALUE

> *A shoe factory sends two marketing scouts to a region of Africa to study the prospects for expanding business.*
> *One sends back a telegram saying: "Situation is hopeless stop no one wears shoes".*
> *The other writes back triumphantly: "Glorious business opportunity stop they have no shoes".*
>
> *— Author unknown*

This story of two marketing scouts represents our story: the same situation elicits different responses, one that captures our hopelessness and the other our hopefulness. The evolving story of diversity as seen and experienced today is both challenging and difficult. Take, for instance, the difference in

215

newspaper headlines from five years ago ("Tolerating the intolerant" (*Montreal Gazette*, March 28, 2010); "We're not all the same" (*Montreal Gazette*, March 14, 2010); "City's face changing rapidly" (Montreal Gazette, March 10, 2010); "Niqab heats up rights controversy" (*Montreal Gazette,* March 3, 2010)) versus today ("Diversity our strength" (*Globe and Mail*, January 26, 2015); "Student show celebrates diversity" (*The Brampton Guardian*, March 12, 2015); "Quebec judge has more latitude than employers; firms must accommodate religious diversity" (*National Post*, March 11, 2015). While we cannot escape what is happening, we do know we can change our response to what is happening. We can, like the second scout, say, "Glorious opportunity —diversity is our new reality."

While our classrooms, offices, and factories are becoming a "rainbow coalition" of people from many different cultures, socio-economic backgrounds, and races, we are still in our infancy in managing, let alone unleashing, the potential that diversity has in store for us. Today 54 percent of Canadian immigrants belong to a visible minority that will rise to 71 percent in 2031 with at least one Canadian in four being foreign born — the highest level since Confederation.

Already, the people we call "minorities" are a numerical majority across the world. By the year 2056, we are told the "average" United States resident will list his/her ancestry as African, Asian, Hispanic, or Arab not white European. In many city school systems, Caucasian students are already a minority in numbers. It simply is a fact — one for which many of us are ill-prepared.

Diversity surrounds us. Our cultural tapestry shows in the things we eat, the tools we use, and the words we speak:

> *Think about our daily routine. A typical Canadian/American*
> *citizen awakens in a bed (an invention from the Near East). After*
> *dressing in clothes (often designed in Italy), he/she eats breakfast*
> *on plates (made in China), eats a banana (grown in Honduras),*
> *and brews coffee (shipped from Nicaragua). And after breakfast,*
> *he/she reads the newspaper (printed by a process invented in*
> *Germany and on paper originally made in China). Then, flips on*
> *a tape recorder (made in Japan) and listens to music (possibly*
> *performed by a band from Cuba).*
>
> -   *Ellis, 1998*

When one reads this, one could not help but chuckle…so true… so delightfully true, and yes — this does represent diversity.

216

"Walk the Line": A Glimpse into How Diversity Is Experienced Today

The topic of diversity was always covered at the beginning of my undergraduate course in Leadership in Small Groups. Due to a growing diverse student composition, I felt that it was important to highlight the impact diversity has in small groups, whether working in one or leading diverse teams. In addition, it needed to be conveyed that they should not leave their ethnicity at the door. To this end, our initial session has habitually included some form of an exercise that allows the students to visually see the diversity of the class. While the experiential learning activity has remained the same, this year saw a new activity emerge, as the teaching team I was working with saw the need to create something that more dynamically illustrated the impact of diversity in workgroups.

The original exercise comprised students placing various colored dots on a large map of the world (indicating their origins as well as the origins of their parents and grandparents). And then verbally share this with the class as a whole. Students were then divided into groups of five to six persons to discuss the following question: "Given your experience and background, how does your cultural origin influence your participation in groups?" The small group discussions that followed were quite animated with students showing high involvement and interest in this activity. The data that was subsequently shared with the class pointed to how national culture influences our values and how values influence our attitudes, which in turn influence our behavior. This powerful data helped students gain insights into how easily judgments are made based on observable behavior, with little appreciation or understanding of why these differences exist. In addition, what surfaced was the realization that while we may come from the same cultural background, we should not leap to the conclusion that everyone in the same culture is the "same".

> *"This powerful data helped students gain insights into how easily judgments are made based on observable behavior... we should not leap to the conclusion that everyone in the same culture is the "same".*

While this exercise did illustrate the diversity of the class, the teaching team felt (after critiquing the exercise) that the impact of diversity being experienced today, with its current broadened definition, was not effectively being highlighted. While students would see where their peers came from, and while dialogue brought out more information, it did not truly capture how diverse these students were. After discussion, it was proposed that a more dynamic process be created to replace the (perhaps) more static one, as it was also deemed necessary to bring to the surface other differences that we may not have readily recognized but experienced. Eventually what emerged was an activity entitled "Walk the Line". This activity consisted of students standing in a line, each facing the same direction. Questions around diversity were asked, and the students would, accordingly, either step *forward* or *backward* depending on their situation surrounding that question. These questions were designed to create a visual and emotional impact. The types of questions, as well as the marked difference in the direction of the steps, contributed to this. Students did not openly express their reaction to certain questions nor the direction

217

the questions required them to take, but many seemed uneasy. At the end of the exercise, students were standing at various distances in the classroom. They were then asked to share their feelings about where they had ended up versus the "original" line they had all stood at. This activity increases in impact the higher the numbers and the larger the physical space, as it allows for a greater range of variations from the original line and, in so doing, dramatizes the differences.

The Diversity Configuration That Emerged

At the front of the class, Ross, one of the students, stated his lack of surprise at where he was located (at the very front). As a tall, white male, he said that while he had not expected to be all the way at the front, he did not feel uncomfortable with his final position. One male student, however, expressed that while he was in the front of the class, he felt as though he was there not because of what he had done, but what his parents and grandparents had accomplished and experienced. This statement was particularly interesting as this student visually did not represent the "norm" of the average white male (he had dreadlocks, large piercings, and numerous tattoos). His statement of not feeling as though his position in the classroom was justified was echoed by many students.

Most of the students in the front did not express surprise, but some did express discomfort at how far they were from their friends and peers. Similarly, the students at the back of the classroom expressed frustration that their accomplishments were not reflected in their positioning, and that their cultural backgrounds should not indicate how "far back" they should be in relation to the others. The teaching assistant for the course was at the back of the class and expressed her feelings on her position as one of frustration and resignation. She explained that although she was a successful individual with a university degree and a coordinator's position at her place of work, she knew that based on her skin color (she was black) she would always be at the back. However, she continued to say that while society may place her at the back, she knew that she was really at the front of the line.

> *"Advancing steps seemed larger than those that put individuals "farther back". Was this due to the fear of being judged or judging others? Were students honest when answering, or did fear and other emotions hold them back?"*

While it was made clear that these questions were merely one method of analyzing diversity, many students seemed affected by the results. The emotions that were raised were very different from those we had seen when using the previous activity: the impact of the diversity was not only visual, but also raised disturbing questions. The size of steps students took seemed to vary according to the direction required to take and question being asked. Advancing steps seemed larger than those that put individuals "farther back". Was this due to the fear of being judged or judging others? Were students honest when answering, or did fear and other emotions hold them back?

The impact of this exercise on the teaching team was clear. When critiquing the session, it was apparent that the activity created drama and visual impact. The statements made further highlighted the emotions the exercise brought forth. The impact on the students was seen and heard through the discussion it created, although the silence of many students might be more telling. This activity gave the community a chance to be aware of the diversity in our class, both hidden and explicit. The questions challenged us to look at how we label others (fat/ thin tall/short, their sexuality, level of education, etc.). While many discussions usually focus on the physical and explicit aspects of diversity, it is important to also address those aspects that may not be as easy to categorize. Asking the students to reflect on the range of diversity in the class helped them recognize that how they see others in the classroom also affects how they see others beyond the classroom — task groups in their work places, the community they live in, and the places they travel to. It also helped them see that while individuals may personally perceive themselves at the front of the line (where they may end up) based on the perception of their peers, and may be entirely different.

> *"... while diversity brings challenges, the possibility of acquiring different skill sets and resources, when com- bined, can create new knowledge and ideas, resulting in a workgroup that is more creative in its product."*

This activity allowed our students the opportunity to examine how they view themselves and others, as well as how they may be perceived by outside forces. While the process may not have been easy, it continued to impact the class over the year. Eventually, some students came to appreciate and recognize that while diversity brings challenges, the possibility of acquiring different skill sets and resources, when combined, can create new knowledge and ideas, resulting in a workgroup that is more creative in its product.

Space Agency/Space Station Diversity in Action: A Rare View Behind the Scenes[1]

The European Space Agency (ESA) is a good example of international cooperation, being an organization of collaboration whose origin is even older than that of the European Union. There are now 18 member countries, with a number of additional countries when including the army of resident contractors at the various branches of the Agency.

Teams are typically very international in nature. There can be as many countries represented as

---

[1] Dr. James Kass, physicist, who works at the European Space Centre, contributed to the following section. His observations cast a useful framework for the management of diversity under certain types of circumstances in an international environment.

members of a team. The common language most often used by a team to communicate with one another, English, may not be the mother tongue of a single team member. Italians will speak together in English so that the French team member can understand. Despite this diversity, the teams generally function very well — the cultural origin of a team member being quite unimportant.

These basic ingredients, more often than not common to all members of a team, ensure that members of teams working on any particular project, despite coming from quite diverse professional backgrounds and nationalities, feel like they make up a homogeneous entity. They have considerably more in common with one another than with other members of their own cultural group outside the Agency, their friends from home, or even their family members.

It is often said that cultural diversity brings rich and different approaches to solving problems and can thus enrich a group. This is probably true. At any rate, coming from different countries, different disciplines, and different organizations, team members certainly can bring a rich diversity to ideas and ways of working to a group.

Of course, as with all seemingly ideal pictures, there are always downsides: some of the

---

KEY INGREDIENTS THAT PROMOTE A HIGH FUNCTIONING TEAM

1.   Common working language: fluency in English (written, spoken, and reading) is required for working at the Agency. Moreover, common spaceflight jargon is used.

2.   High-level education: All team members are university graduates, often with two or more degrees of higher education behind them.

3.   Common basic interest: those joining the Agency usually have a deep interest in all things to do with space flight.

4.   Similar economic standing: members of staff (and resident con- tractors) earn good salaries (above that of local professionals or civil servants with similar education).

5.   Similar consequences for failure or mistakes.

6.   Diversity of cultural background is common to all — all staff feel like expatriates, even those few locals, who are a small minority in the very international atmosphere.

FIGURE X-7

---

ingredients listed are not quite commonly shared in a healthy manner; some employees are indeed "more equal than others", e.g., permanent staff have job security, possibilities for professional advancement; and some special privileges, which temporary contractors (making up almost half the staff at the Agency) do not share. Moreover, a fairly rigid and pronounced hierarchal structure can contribute to lack of openness and diminished freedom to speak one's mind, when the division or section head is too strong-headed. These factors can diminish the quality of the key ingredients listed above and result in de-motivation and diminished quality of work.

Nevertheless, all told, professional and cultural diversity at the Agency can and does provide a healthy atmosphere and good teamwork provided that there are sufficient key ingredients shared in common.

In the next section, James Kass, who was acquainted with all the parties cited below and having worked closely with most of them in his capacity of training them to perform experiments in space, writes the following about his observations about diversity in space.

James Kass: Diversity in Orbital Space Flight

Although members of the teams building the rockets, preparing the scientific payloads, and those in the ground-operations teams can go home to their families in the evenings or at least after some days' work, this is not the case for the teams working and living together and isolated in orbit around the Earth (or the Moon) — or, in the future, on a journey to Mars. Some of these orbital teams have been quite diverse, culturally and professionally, in Soviet/Russians-led missions, NASA-led missions, and, finally, on the International Space Station (ISS). It is rather more difficult to assess the quality of a space team's functioning because there is little documented information; this is especially sensitive with an international team and/or culturally diverse team members. Anecdotal information, however, always exists, and this can certainly be drawn on.

The Soviets often flew non-Russian Eastern Block citizens on their flights, as well as some other countries' citizens; but an interesting period began when NASA paid the Russians a goodly sum for flying American astronauts on the MIR (Russian) space station. The relationship was sensitive because, in principle, rather than an equal collaboration, one organization (NASA) was paying the other for a service. Most of the time this was quite successful with few hitches related to the diverse crew and their customer-service provider relationship.

There were some exceptions, one of which has been well-documented and is worth noting here. Jerry Linenger, an American astronaut on the MIR station, was an example of a crew member who behaved in a manner that underlined some sensitive ingredients that were key, but not quite commonly shared. He was the customer, and he proudly and stubbornly carried out his job as a good American astronaut should without much respect or adaptation to the working and living culture of the Russian cosmonauts on the MIR station. When a leak occurred on the station causing a problem with ventilation and the crew were advised to stop exercising, Linenger refused to cooperate: the Americans were paying the Russians for a service, and the latter should deliver and he (Linenger) needed exercise to keep healthy.

(Next Page) — — — — — — — — — — — — — — →

For the Russian crew (Tsibliyev and Lazutkin), who were working hard trying to mend the leak, this was not understandable and certainly was not an example of a team holding together. Linenger did not have much confidence in his Russian team members and was critical about their handling of the difficult situation, both while in orbit and after the mission. Here was a relationship of un-equals — the customer and the service provider; this need not have been a problem, but under pressure, and with some difficult characters, the ingredient of inequality of members of the team can certainly lead to problems.

A very different example occurred during a visit to the MIR station mission, refusing to say anything detrimental about his colleagues. Another key ingredient that was different for each crew was the consequence of failure: for the Russian team members, mistakes made could tally against their end-of-mission bonus, which was of great importance for the well-being of their families for years to come; the consequences for the "international" crew were rather milder. Different consequences for different team members can certainly affect behavior and stress very differently, which can (but need not) lead to a lack of cohesion and common goals.

Another example of a key ingredient that was different for each crew was the living accommodation at Star City, where the crew trained and lived. The Russian, European, and American crew lived there, but there were major differences in the comforts of life. Whereas the Russians lived in cramped, standard, simple apartments, the Americans stood out in that they had large and comfortable American-style houses purposely built for them so they could "feel at home". This certainly did not contribute positively toward team spirit; instead it underlined the economic and cultural differences of the team members. It may be noted that the European astronauts' living quarters (in the "Profilactorium") were not much more comfortable than that of their Russian colleagues.

On a positive note, the new era of the ISS has certainly launched a period of healthier Russian–American collaboration. Teams of three are usually alternately headed by an American or by a Russian, both contributing toward transport and building of the commonly used station. In principle, this certainly works toward a healthier atmosphere of teamwork.

In looking over these "Diversity in Action" examples, I was reminded of a possible implication for leveraging diversity, namely screening and selecting team candidates on the basis of their competence in handling diversity along with other professional criteria. When I showed the international company the "Making Differences Matter" example, one of the owners reported that this competence in utilizing diversity was so important that staff who couldn't do it were let go.

Making Differences Matter

These past three years I have been a consultant to a profit-making organization that places a high value on learning and personal growth among its workers. I was originally called in to help facilitate dialogue between plant and office managers. The owners had a high respect for their managers, recognizing their hard work and loyalty. When I first met the managers I was struck by the wide range of diversity I was confronted with. This group of 12 persons represented a rich array of diversity: multi-discipline, multinational, multi-racial, multilingual, multi-educational, and multi-religious. They came from different backgrounds: Russian, Portuguese, American, Jamaican, Indian, Guyanese, Polish, Chinese, and Jewish. They had different religions: Unitarian, Sikh, Orthodox Christian, Hindu, Anglican, Catholic, and Jewish. Their education ranged from high school to master's degree. There was diversity at every level. What a group — a real powerhouse.

Over the three years, I set up self-directed interdependent project groups that were mutually beneficial to both the plant and the office. They set their focus, their team composition, meeting times, and their criteria for success. Trust and respect for each other developed, coaching teams voluntarily emerged, and results were celebrated. They took initiative to "green-light" open discussions. It was powerful.

The success was influenced by several things: the organization's leaders, in this case the owners, had worked hard to define "belonging" in terms of a set of values and a clear sense of purpose. They had worked hard to fully tap the human resource potential of every member of their management workforce, managing disparate talents to achieve common goals. They had also managed to transcend what organizational leaders fear most from diversity — the lowering of standards and a sense that "anything goes". They had managed through hard work (trial and error), clear vision, and openness to develop a genuine workplace of diversity:

- They understood that a diverse workforce needs to embody different perspectives, opinions, and insights.
- They had created an organizational culture of high standards of performance.
- They had a well-articulated and widely understood mission.
- They were able to create a culture where their workers felt valued and respected.
- They delegated, listened, and understood differences.
- They had created a culture that encourages personal growth and development.
- They began to see the need for open discussion and trust between different departments and had set things in motion for this to happen.

Prior to the last management retreat, one of the owners met with four representatives of the management team to ask them for feedback about the previous retreat and input about the upcoming retreat. Their feedback and input indicated their trust in the process and their belief that their feedback would be heard. Their desired focus for the retreat was "leadership and communication". Their feedback to me was, "a less crowded schedule" and more time to "network". They got both.

V. PERSONAL THOUGHTS

My experience as a faculty member teaching about groups and leadership has taught me a few sobering lessons about technology and its impact on group functioning as well as the subtle, inherent dynamics of, emotional intelligence and diversity in groups.

What I have noticed is that when teams are formed on a spontaneous, voluntary, or involuntary basis, diversity issues play a subtle role: how a student is welcomed into a group that is already formed, how a group member is listened to, how a group member's ideas are given attention to, or even how a group member is given feedback. While there are a myriad of other dynamics underlying these responses, such as personality differences and willingness or ability to take on responsibility, unspoken elements of diversity (age, sex, status, culture, socio-economic background, education, etc.) play a role in influencing a team's cohesiveness, trust, flexibility, and/or capacity to leverage its resources and skills.

As educators, coaches, and consultants in the field of "Human Systems", we have a serious task ahead that may seem paradoxical, but in reality is not: preserving the human touch, whilst celebrating the magnificence of what technology and diversity have opened up for us and has in store for us.

VI. CARPE DIEM - SEIZE THE DAY

> *At the end of all thought must be action.*
> -   *Aldous Huxley*

Seize the day! Give it all you've got! How true! Yet how hard to do!

It is hard to imagine what the contents of this book will mean to different people who choose to read it. Some will read this book as part of an assignment for a course in which they have been asked to select a theory to analyze their group. Nothing more, nothing less. Having completed the assignment they move on to other things often forgetting the links they may have made between theory and practice.

Others will read this book and find it hard to identify with it, let alone find meaning with any of the theories presented, any of the concepts raised and/or any of the processes discussed. The book gets put aside, only to be retrieved, when and if the next occasion calls for its perusal. Nothing more, nothing less.

For still others, this book will be read, even reread with some caution, curiosity and ambivalence. The readers may agree with what they've read, may even begin to appreciate the fine line between content and process, the relationship between work and emotion and the role of conflict in groups. While their curiosity gets deepened with what they have understood, this understanding does not translate into action. Nothing more, nothing less.

However, for some people, this book will open up a new way of viewing things, spark a new perspective on old issues, create a renewed understanding of familiar concepts and instill a deeper appreciation of how reflection can lend meaning to action. In short, for these people a powerful and indelible shift will have taken place - one in which groups are viewed as living systems capable of change and growth, one in which members are perceived as colleagues to collaborate with and not as colleagues to compete against and one in which the whole is experienced as greater than the sum of its parts. These learners are on a journey, open to influence and be influenced, open to leadership and followership alike and open to propel things forward with integrity and a search for excellence.

The following is a poignant story that Stephen Covey tells about himself and his encounter with an experience that was incongruent with his expectation. It is worth repeating for his encounter led to an unexpected paradigm shift.

> I remember a mini-paradigm shift I experienced one Sunday morning on a subway in New York. People were sitting quietly - some reading newspapers, some lost in thought, some resting with their eyes closed. It was a calm, peaceful scene.
>
> Then suddenly, a man and his children entered the subway car. The children were so loud and rambunctious that instantly the whole climate changed.
>
> The man sat down next to me and closed his eyes, apparently oblivious to the situation. The children were yelling back and forth, throwing things, even grabbing people's papers. It was very disturbing. And yet, the man sitting next to me did nothing.
>
> It was difficult not to feel irritated. I could not believe that he could be so insensitive as to let his children run wild like that and do nothing about it, taking no responsibility at all. It was easy to see that everyone else on the subway felt irritated, too. So finally, with what I felt was unusual patience and restraint, I turned to him and said, "Sir, your children are really disturbing a lot of people. I wonder if you couldn't control them a little more?"
>
> The man lifted his gaze as if to come to a consciousness of the situation for the first time and said softly, "Oh, you're right. I guess I should do something about it. We just came from the hospital where their mother died about an hour ago. I don't know what to think, and I guess they don't know how to handle it either."
>
> Can you imagine what I felt at that moment? My paradigm shifted. Suddenly I saw things differently, and because I saw differently, I thought differently, I felt differently, I behaved differently.

Taken from "The 7 Habits of Highly Effective People"
by Stephen Covey (1989, pp. 30,31).

What a powerful and compelling paradigm shift. My hope is that in grasping the essence of what this book represents, you the reader, will begin to see things differently about groups, think things differently about groups, feel things differently about groups and most importantly do things differently in groups.

PERSONAL NOTES

REFERENCES

Goleman, D. (2006). *Social Intelligence*. New York: Bantam Books.

Goleman, D. (1998). *What makes a leader?* Harvard Business Review, Nov-Dec.

Goleman, D. (1998). *Working with Emotional Intelligence*. New York: Bantam Dell.

Hare, P.A. (1976). *Handbook of Small Group Research*, (2nd ed.) New York: Free Press.

Helgesen, S. (1990). *The Female Advantage: Women's Ways of Leadership*. New York: Bantam-Doubleday.

Hersey, P., Blanchard, K., & Johnson, D.E. (2007). *Management of Organizational Behaviour: Leading Human Resources*. Englewood Cliffs, NJ: Prentice-Hall.

Janis, I. (1972). *Victims of Groupthink: A Psychological Study of Foreign-Policy Decisions and Fiascoes*. Boston, MA: Houghton.

Johnson, B. (1996). *Polarity Management: Identifying and Managing Unsolvable Problems*, (2nd ed.) Human Resource Development Press.

Kass, R., Kass, J., Binder, H., & Kraft, N. (2010). Conflict handling modes of three crews during a 264-day Space Flight Simulation. *Journal of Aviation, Space, and Environmental Medicine, 81(5)*, 502-505.

Kass, R., Kass, J. (2001). Psychological Training for Small Groups. *Medico-biological and Psychological Studies in the Experiment with Extended Isolation*. International Conference, Russian Academy of Medical Sciences, June 5-6, Moscow, Russia.

Kass, R., Kass, J. (2001). Teamwork During Long-Term Isolation: SFINCSS Experiment P-006. In *Simulation of Extended Isolation: Advances and Problems*. Institute of Biomedical Problems, Moscow, Russia, (2001), 124-47.

Kass, R., Kass, J. (2001). Teamwork-Work During Long Duration Isolation. 52nd International Astronautical Congress. October 1-5, Toulouse, France.

Kass, R., Kass, J. 1994. Understanding small group behaviour with a view to maximizing team effectiveness and task accomplishment. In CAPSULS, *a 7 day space mission simulation. Final report and scientific results (Sponsored by the Canadian Space Agency)*, held on January 20-27, 1994, at the Defense and Civil Institute of Environmental Medicine. Toronto, Ontario.

Lencioni, P. (2002). *The Five Dysfunctions of a Team*. San Francisco: Jossey Bass.

Mintzberg, H. (1980). *The Nature of Managerial Work*. New York: Harper & Row.

Napier, R., Gershenfeld, M. (1989). *Groups: Theory and Experience*, (4th ed.) Boston: Houghton Mifflin.

Sandy, P. (1994). *Choosing the Right Stuff*. Westport, CT: Praeger Publishers.

Zander, A. (1982). *Making Groups Effective*. San Francisco: Jossey-Bass.